CREATING
YOUR
GIANT SELF

FURTHER CONSPIRACIES

If you would like to read further on the New Age Conspiracy to elevate Man's consciousness on this planet and elsewhere, get the following titles from your book dealer:

Undoing Yourself With Energized Meditation
    by Christopher S. Hyatt, Ph.D.
Secrets of Western Tantra, The Sexuality of the Middle Path by Christopher S. Hyatt, Ph.D.
Cosmic Trigger by Robert Anton Wilson
Cosmic Trigger II by Robert Anton Wilson
Prometheus Rising by Robert Anton Wilson
Quantum Psychology by Robert Anton Wilson
Ishtar Rising by Robert Anton Wilson
The New Inquisition by Robert Anton Wilson
Coincidance by Robert Anton Wilson
Neuropolitique by T. Leary and Robert Anton Wilson
Info-Psychology by Timothy Leary
Angel Tech, A Modern Shaman's Guide to Reality Selection by Antero Alli
The Shaman Warrior by Gini Graham Scott
Zen Without Zen Masters by Camden Benares
A Handful of Zen by Camden Benares
What You Should Know About The Golden Dawn by Israel Regardie
Healing Energy, Prayer and Relaxation by Israel Regardie

And to get your free catalog of all of our titles, write to:

New Falcon Publications
Catalog Dept.
3660 N 3rd Street
Phoenix, AZ 85012 U.S.A.

CREATING YOUR GIANT SELF

BY

Robert Rose, Ph.D.

Foreword By
Robert Anton Wilson

1990
NEW FALCON PUBLICATIONS
(FALCON PRESS)
PHOENIX, ARIZONA U.S.A.

International Standard Book Number: 0-941404-61-7

First Edition 1990

Book Design, Typography and Production by
Cameron, Holmes, and Stone

NEW FALCON PUBLICATIONS
3660 N 3rd Street
Phoenix, Arizona 85012 U.S.A.
(602) 246-3546

Manufactured in the United States of America

TABLE OF CONTENTS

Part Three
Creating Your Giant Self

Foreword

Robert Anton Wilson, Ph.D.

I am not a labor leader. I would not lead you into the Promised Land if I could, because if I could lead you in, somebody else could lead you out. -- **Eugene V. Debs**

We are only ten years away from the 21st Century, but most people are still living intellectually in the Dark Ages: hunting for "witches" and other servitors of Satan is our new national sport. Those who believe in automatic Progress should seriously reflect on that. In the grim days of Senator Joe McCarthy, bad as they were, "witch-hunting" was only a metaphor, but now it is again a literal fact.

We put men on the moon over 20 years ago, split the atom nearly 50 years ago, and learned the facts of evolution almost 150 years ago.

We have begun entering the age of genetic engineering and nano-technology, we are four decades into the Information Age, some of our rockets have left the solar system and sail now in an ocean of stars -- but the Federal Communications Commission has a list of Taboo Words just like that of any other stone age tribe, the Supreme Court believes that some metaphysical Platonic entity called "obscenity" can inhabit a book the way a ghost allegedly inhabits a haunted house, and most Americans are not sure, according to a recent poll, if the earth revolves around the sun once a day or once a year.

H. G. Wells wrote, in 1922, that modern history is a race between education and catastrophe. The remark became more obviously true, for most of us, after August 6, 1945, but education has not therefore improved, and in many dimensions appears to have dis-improved (as the English say.) A planet of mental pygmies led by a deluded and/or cynical politicians, gripped by paleolithic superstitions and blind prejudices, plunges recklessly along, with the tools of Armageddon (or Utopia) in its ignorant hanks and a weird variety of bats, barn owls and semantic spooks in the cranial area where its brain should be. As I wrote in *Illuminatus*, we are a race of potential giants who have been forced to live in midget's huts and have developed a habitual mental crouch, which we call "respect for authority."

1

This book attempts to awaken the sleeping giant within each of us. It offers liberation for the enslaved, enlightenment for those who live in darkness, aid and comfort for those who seek truth in a world of hypocrisy and deceit, tonic doses of hope for those who have succumbed to despair. Naturally, one can expect such a much-needed and useful book to be denounced by educators, journalist, politicians, "experts" of all stripe, and -- **aber naturlich!** -- especially by the rev. clergy.

If we are truncated giants, pitiful shadows of what we might have become -- if the world is still at its dawn and we have never seen a true Man, as Emerson once wrote -- this must be attributed to the fact that we are led by shepherds who want their sheep to remain docile and submissive. It would be pleasant to think that the shepherds only intend to shear us. Some of us, however, have looked down the road, spied the abattoir, and like Gurdjieff, no longer believe in the myth of the "Good" Shepherd. We know the herdsmen are allied with the butchers.

Strong words? Well, this is not your ordinary Self Help book. It does not claim all our problems can be solved by wishful thinking and soothing mantras. It recognizes that we are in a Penal colony and the only escape lies in being smart enough and tough enough to outwit the warden and the prison guards -- especially the **internal warden and internal guards,** the imprints in our brains left by our well-meaning parents and teachers.

Dr. Rose is not peddling Positive Thinking, Pop Hinduism, Transcendental Masturbation or any of the other usual ingredients in New Age books. He is trying to explain, in simple Basic English, how **you** got mechanized -- diminished -- by hardwired genetic programs, early imprints, Pavlovian conditioning, abominable miseducation, and an economic system that demands that people become robots in order to serve it. He then offers you some tools to use in what will be a life-long struggle to de-robotize yourself. He does not pretend that the struggle will be less than life-long or that he has a few Magic Formulas that you can memorize which will solve all your problems forever.

In other words, Diogenes can put out his lantern and go home. Here, by god, in the plain light of day is an honest man.

Of course, such a book has no value at all for those of you who are already mentally, emotionally and spiritually free of the Pavlovian mechanisms that control the rest of humanity. Having achieved perfection, you don't need to work on yourself anymore. If you are a member of a Fundamentalist church, or a Marxist political party, or the Committee for Scientific Investigation of Claims of the Paranormal, you already know that most people are pretty stupid and that only you and your friends see things objectively and realistically. You don't need this book, and you will only find it offensive. Rose actually suggests that none of us has achieved perfect error-free rationality yet, and that we all need to make a mighty effort to liberate ourselves from the shackles of intellectual dogma and emotional rigidity. Obviously, he means everybody else but **you**, right?

Well...maybe you have some doubts. Maybe you have noticed that, once in a while, you are almost as dumb as other people. Maybe you've been embarrassed at times to observe that old childish programs, which you thought you had outgrown, still rear up and take control of you...occasionally. (Not as often as they control other people, of course, and certainly not nearly as much as they control your boss, your spouse, your ex-spouse and those idiots who vote for the Other Political Party.)

Maybe, even if you know the earth takes a year, not a day, to orbit the sun, you are not quite sure whether "God" or "ESP" are real or imaginary, or if monogamy is really suitable for everybody, or why even the most intelligent people can be "hurt" -- emotionally wounded, in painful ways -- by merely verbal put-downs.

If you recognize any of these doubts, misgivings or philosophical perplexities in yourself, Dr. Rose is the man for you. He will not give you dogmatic answers of Guaranteed Results In Ten Easy Steps; but he will give you a great deal of the intellectual ammunition you need to begin working on these basic existential problems and realistically seeking the trade-offs and make-shifts that will work for you, for a while, in your particular predicament. He will also show you how to abandon each trade-off or make-shift when it no longer works, and how to build a better one to replace it. Remember: he is teaching you a process of growth, not selling a Conjure John Tonic that will cure all the ills of man and beast.

Those who are aware of what modern science has discovered since about 1900 know the following facts, which, if they had been available to the founders of our religions, our political institutions, our educational system and our corporations, would certainly have radically changed the social world that they created -- the world that was dumped on us before we were even born.

1. We belong to a primate species. Our genes carry all the standard primate "instincts" or programs. We did not "fall" from Eden, but evolved from ordinary mammals, controlled by ordinary mammalian drives.

2. We have brains that are programmed by chemical bonds which depend on our genetic inheritance, our early imprints, our conditioning and our diet (among other factors.) No two people have exactly the same blend of chemicals programming their brains, so no two people ever perceive the same "reality." The genetic-imprinted-conditioned-dietary differences between the brain chemistry of Mr. Abel, sober, and Ms. Baker, sober, are often just as great as those between Mr. Cox., tripping on LSD, Ms. Dawkins, drunk on a quart of whiskey, Mr. Evans, wired on cocaine and Ms. Franklin, laid back and stoned on marijuana. The chemicals in our brains determine what we experience, and we all have different hormonal and neurochemical programs.

3. Misunderstandings between people are therefore inevitable, and will tend to become bitter, protracted or even violent if nobody understands the relativity of brain chemistry and the consequent relativity of perceived reality-tunnels. Dogmatists, whether they be religious, political or "scientific," all make the mistake of thinking everybody is seeing, or should be seeing, the "same" world **they** see; but everybody is seeing (sensing, feeling, experiencing) their own unique world.

4. Such misunderstandings will remain even if people learn the facts of neurological relativity, but in the latter case conflicts will be less bitter, less protracted and can be intelligently negotiated. When you understand why your boss, full of testosterone and adrenaline, does not see things like your wife, full of female hormones, you can deal with both of them better, without thinking that either they are both idiots or you are the idiot because you do not see what they see.

5. All systems of dogma contradict these neuro-chemical facts and survive only because of mis-education (ignorance) or because of "deliberate stupidity" -- Arthur Koestler's phrase -- i.e. a decision to ignore what is known about brain-relativity and still try to force everybody to agree with, or at least submit to, one's own idiosyncratic reality-tunnel. It is very difficult to decide how much of the dogma still surviving in our 1990's world results from mere ignorance of neurology, and how much is "deliberate stupidity" in Koestler's sense -- that is, raw lust for power and stubborn refusal to face the facts. In a sense, it doesn't matter. What matters is that we are trapped in a world full of people who want us to deny our own senses and pretend to see what they see, and we have to fight every day to avoid being browbeaten or brainwashed into losing our own eyes and actually falling into the group hypnosis of seeing what the Shepherd tells the herd to see.

6. The struggle against this group hypnosis is the longest-lasting war in human history, and in a sense is history. Virtually all religions, most schools and a large segment of economic institutions are governed by persons who either do not know the facts of neurochemical relativity, or who have chosen in "deliberate stupidity" to ignore these facts and try to force the rest of us to adjust to their own favorite reality-grids. In the attempt to adjust to these religions, schools and economic institutions, most of us have been partially crippled -- we have "**literally** taken leave of our senses and have **laterally** been robbed blind," as Dr. Timothy Leary likes to say. That is, we have surrendered what we see and feel and experience and have tried to live by the definitions of our Masters.

In Dr. Rose's metaphor, we have lost our potential Giant Selves and become the Diminished Selves that our Masters wish us to be in order to serve the institutions they have created. We are supposed to remain docile sheep, remember?

To "come back to our senses" and **see** again -- to "wake up and smell the coffee" -- cannot be learned in one week-end of slick semi Esalen semi-yogic gimmicks. You can only **begin** the process in such a week-end. To regain the full potentials of free thought, free action, emotional flexibility, sensory awareness and joyful creativity which you lost while learning to be "adjusted," you will have to work hard and work for the rest of your life.

The only thing that makes it bearable to confront this diagnosis of "the horror of the situation on Planet Earth" (Gurdjieff's phrase") is that when you begin such work -- organizing your own jail break -- you discover that each step forward opens a whole new world to you, a world you never saw before, a New-Found-Land full of Zen beauty and surrealist mystery...and each succeeding step takes you into still another, stranger, more wonderful New Heaven and New Earth.

The human mind is not born when the body is born. A truly human mind takes a lifetime to be born.

Still, a lifetime spent in learning to be born -- to be alive, not a mechanism; to be laughing most of the time and not whining most of the time; to be learning daily and not just repeating formulas like a parrot -- well, that is something only a human, and no other animal, can experience. It is worth the hard work and the effort, after all. Everybody who's tried it agrees. It is comfortable in the pasture with the other sheep, but there's a lot more fun when you escape the herdsmen and their abattoirs.

Now, let Dr. Rose give you the first navigational markers to guide you out of the womb, down the vaginal canal, toward the birth of a free mind...

Introduction

Welcome to my reality! It is the only one I know, but it is merely one of many possibilities. My reality may or may not be better then yours. I'm certain that it is different. It has taken me many years to clarify and define my reality because so many people and institutions have confused me. Most of these people and institutions had no evil plan for trying to mold me into their versions of reality. Many sincerely believed that what they did was in my best interests. Some things they did were. Others seriously damaged my self-confidence and limited my personal growth.

I reached a point where I was tired of being lied to, of being hyped by hucksters in religious and academic robes, each of whom assured me that if I followed his way I would be free and fulfilled. I make no such unrealistic and impossible promises to you. The universe and human beings are not simple and therefore complex solutions are necessary.

If you are looking for simple solutions there are an abundance of self-help books that have easy how-to-do-it formats. Each will offer you something neatly packaged so that you do not have to think nor examine your motives, emotions, and life. You will feel good for awhile and then you will again be overwhelmed by the complexities of life.

I offer you a book that doesn't try to make you feel good, but instead strips away all the facades created by yourself, others, and our institutions until you see yourself as you are! Pretty frightening?

You are frightened because you have been convinced that the real you is not valuable or lovable. This is not true. The real you is so much greater than anything you've ever thought of that you will be furious that you let your parents, teachers, friends, and the institutions of our society convince you otherwise. They convinced you that the diminished self that they helped create is the real you. I want to help you see that your real self, your giant self, is just waiting to emerge.

All this cannot be explained in a magazine article. It cannot be resolved by positive thinking,(which is usually a denial of thinking.) You must examine and think. You need some data and concepts. You don't need to agree with me, but in order to disagree you must read, think, and then base your arguments on something besides what your mother, teacher, or religious leader told you was true.

This doesn't mean that my reality is based solely on so-called scientific fact. Rational thinking, logic, and statistics are only tools for thinking. Such tools are only as good as the tool-user. There is an equal place in my reality for feeling and intuition and other non-linear, non-predominantly left-brained types of problem-solving, although these are also subject to error and are imperfect, just like logic.

My giant self tells me that there is only uncertainty. I wish there was certainty and permanent security, but I believe these are illusions that lead to errors and disillusionment.

My giant self often doesn't function as I wish. I don't want my wife, children, friends, or those I work with to be angry or disappointed with me, so instead of compromising, which is an expression of my giant self, I capitulate, give in. This is my diminished self fearfully expressing itself.

There are times that I take a particular and temporary stance because I don't have the emotional or mental strength or stamina to deal with the situation. If I am choosing my battleground carefully and thoughtfully, it is my giant self in action. I may be entering a battle knowing the other persons are equally certain that what they believe is right. Each of us sees things from his own reality and my giant self can work with another's so that each gains something. I realize and accept that each of us will have to lose something of value so the other does not feel cheated.

One of the things I hope you will learn is how to get into the other person's reality so that the two of you can come to a reasonable, livable compromise. There are no situations in which you can be a total winner when another human being is, or believes he is, a total loser.

I discovered my giant self because I was tired of living in fear. Fear has so many faces that it is often difficult to recognize its forms, but its crippling effects are felt. There are things that you should be or need to be afraid of, so living without fear leads to certain disaster. Fear, like pain, can be seen as a warning, a useful indicator that something is wrong.

Understanding your fears, as well as your errors, can be useful in improving the quality of your life. The quality of your life will improve in direct proportion to how much of your security you are willing to risk. This does not mean courting danger blindly for the thrill of it, but rather constantly challenging what you believe because growth means stretching beyond your present boundaries.

The weight-lifter constantly reaches plateaus. He thinks he can lift nothing heavier. He has to make some change. It may be a nutritional change, a different schedule or coach, or emotionally he must be able to push himself one step further beyond his present pain barrier. He must take a chance, risk failure and disaster, and fight his fears and the pain involved. There is no growth without risk and it usually entails pain and coping with fear.

So, welcome to my reality! In it there are no final answers or truths, but rather a process, a means to consciously create your own reality. People who have found truths and answers have always been followed by others who have modified their teaching. The same will happen to me. The concepts that are most applicable to this era will be used by you as they have been by me. The world will continue to change and some of these ideas will be replaced by others developed by some other people who have the courage to dissect themselves and their culture.

This will occur because in every solution or set of solutions, there lie the seeds of the next problem. This is the nature of finite solutions. There is a temporariness about them, just as there is a physical mortality for each of us.

Welcome to my reality, which is built on the absolute certainty of uncertainty. Which is built upon the absolute security that security is an illusion.

There is no permanent escape from uncertainty, insecurity, errors, and fears. However, you can use these rather than be immobilized by them. Psychological defense mechanisms are useful in temporarily dealing with your fears. But if you repress, sublimate, or project your fears without ever facing or understanding them, you will have lived your life controlled by them.

I have read book after book, gone to many seminars by erudite men and women, briefly followed various gurus, hoping to find the answer to lead me to security, certainty, and inner peace. They anesthetized my brain, mind, body, and soul, but my fears remained or returned.

Strangely enough, now that I have faced and better understand my human fallibility, it is much easier to live with. I am not without fears, insecurities, and I make all kinds of avoidable mistakes, but I understand them, forgive myself and others whose errors affect me, and I go on with life. I am much happier than I have ever been.

The same can happen to you, but not without sweat, blood, and tears. The books and gurus who promised me the world on a silver platter if I just followed their teachings, left me empty and hungry. I will help you onto a path and give you a process of self-discovery that is not easy, but will nourish you. It does not give you bread, but teaches you how to bake.

We stand at the threshold of controlling the evolution of our species. To do this we must take responsibility for our lives and our planet. First, we must overcome four million years of evolution which places each person's individual needs for survival secondary to the needs of the planet and species. Second, we must listen to our bodies, minds, and spirits to determine what really is our true nature. Most of us don't know and we spout our words, ideas, and attitudes based on our fears and ignorance.

Our brains have proven to have a plasticity far beyond what we have believed them to have. Our institutions have molded us in ways that seemed best for the species, but have allowed us to place ourselves and the planet in jeopardy.

I believe we can consciously change ourselves and our institutions and make a world in which all that is beautiful, kind, thoughtful, intelligent, and courageous in humanity will become the rule and all that is ugly, stupid, venal, and evil will not be tolerated.

If you allow yourself through your will, courage, knowledge, and choices seriously to enter into my reality you will be frightened, confused, and even angry. If you reread, think through, and persist until you open up to these thoughts, you may experience the happiness, the ecstasy I felt and continue to feel through this process of discovery.

Welcome to my reality. Knowledge, self-honesty, and courage will enable you to detect what is real and unreal for you so that you can live with and use the uncertainty and fear which seem to be the result of our vulnerability, our humanness, our mortality.

Welcome. Take my hand. We will enter the darkness together as we search for the light.

Part One

The Diminished Self

One

Case History:
How Schools Destroy Students

Curiosity and the desire to learn and understand appear to be the natural outcome of having a nervous system. The more complex the brain and nervous system the more curious the animal is about itself, others, and its environment. The urge to know and explore continues throughout an animal's life -- unless this urge is disturbed, distorted, or destroyed.

Children are curious little animals who want to learn, but something happens to them before they get to school and is worsened when they are there. I will discuss how the family creates the diminished self and, sadly, schools continue this destructive process.

Think about it: If schools stimulated and encouraged children's creativity and learning, students would be asking for longer days, shorter lunches, and fewer holidays. They wouldn't be hiding in forests and drain pipes, getting sick at 8:00 A.M., and purposely creating situations which cause them to be suspended or expelled. They wouldn't be dropping out at a rate of forty to fifty per cent of potential graduates. Something is very wrong and it's not just with the children.

In the beginning of American schooling going to school was a privilege, an opportunity. In every society there had been two major classes, the ruling elite which included the rulers, the priesthood, and the military leaders and the lower class which included the rest of that society. Schools help to create a middle class and also to perpetuate the lower class. Schooling enabled the immigrants to quickly learn English. For those with the requisite abilities schools enabled them to get out of the lower class.

Industrialization meant people were treated like machines and children were used the same way. A child who was allowed to go to school was often saved from either brutal factory work or equally exhausting farm work. Most of the children did at least some work in conjunction with their schooling.

With the opportunity to go to school full-time a child had the chance to escape a lifetime of numbing physical labor. He also was allowed to explore the knowledge then available. Yet even then, except for a few pockets of Socratic instruction, usually reserved for the children of the rich, schooling was teacher-directed, rigid, and totally authoritarian. The teacher may have been an economic slave to the local school board, but he was the absolute master of the children. Children who were unable to learn were weeded out and those who could learn were cowed or beaten into submission. As bad as that sounds it was preferable to factory or farm work.

Schooling was not mandatory for everyone. Minorities in general, Blacks, Mexicans, Chinese, and Indians were often forbidden to go to school or they were marginally educated in segregated schools. As recently as 1964, ten miles from my home, a district had one Black school and one for Mexican-Americans. The Black school was in the Black ghetto, but the Mexican-American students were bused from all over town.

One reason that schooling is not successful is that racism and ignorance are still rampant. Good economic times make it less obvious and insidious, but in bad times a decent life is difficult, if not impossible, for minorities. Many minorities, which include the most poorly schooled whites, comprise the lower economic class - the poor. Being poor, they cannot afford the things the other classes take for granted such as adequate nutritious food, warm and clean shelter, a job that gives some satisfaction and feeling of worth, and adequate medical and health care. When these poor children were working or in separate schools (and before TV) they had little awareness of how others actually lived. They didn't expect much from life.

With desegregation (not integration, because it takes much more than sending children to the same schools to integrate them), they have a clear idea of the differences in their lives from those of their schoolmates. Yet, if the poorer students keep up in dress, food, and material things with their more affluent neighbors they place a burden on their families' budgets. When they don't keep up they are teased. Physical and dental handicaps are also cause for teasing. It's even worse for the poor within their own groups. They scapegoat and cannibalize one another because it's safer than striking out at the middle class students.

Schools are really battlegrounds in a civil war based on class differences and opportunities. In schools where minorities are the majority those with minor access to the affluent life are predators upon each other. Those in the majority who point to the minorities who have "made it" and chastise those who haven't as parasites, drones, and failures have no idea of how the odds are so stacked up against the majority of the poor.

Besides the lack of many of the basic necessities of life available to most middle class children, the poor often live in homes where life is lived on the cutting edge of chaos and disintegration. They live in crime-infested neighborhoods because crime is one of the main ways many of the brighter and more powerful members of their communities survive. They thrive within their own communities by making the average person's already difficult life more miserable. The parents are frightened, exhausted, depressed, and have little hope. Their children seldom can escape or overcome these feelings and often bring them into the classroom.

What is happening now is similar to the caste system in India. The poor are the Untouchables. They are trapped in a vicious cycle of poverty and dependency and are kept there by the schools and other social institutions supposedly pledged to help them escape this cycle. Those who run these institutions honestly believe they are helping the poor, which is why these leaders are so dangerous. It is a situation of good people doing bad things to other good people. The privileged good people do not realize that they have a vested interest in keeping the caste system alive. Their religions, the media, and the government keep their patronizing attitude alive and perpetuate the myth of opportunity for the poor.

Schools try to ignore the physical, mental, and emotional traumas poor children live with and expect them to be interested in a curriculum that is fine for a WASP, but not for a barrio or ghetto child. These children bring the noise, chaos, and disruptions of their environments into the schools which makes the schooling for all less effective.

The fact that minority children create a disproportionate amount of the problems in the schools further fuels the prejudice and anger of the majority. As usual, the victim is blamed for his problems. In a program I taught dealing with high-risk students only one per cent were middle class; 99% were poor. This was true of almost three hundred referred 6th, 7th, and 8th graders in three years. Schools reflect and support the racism and class prejudice of our society.

One reason that this continues is that our stated ideals and goals are so different from our practices. We honestly believe in equality, justice, and fairness. We are not evil people and we feel that we are doing everything to give everyone equal access to the limited resources. And, more than any other people we have striven and are still striving to do better. But we should look carefully at our schools and their failures to see what we need to do to come closer to our high ideals.

Even if you are a WASP, the schools do not encourage your giant self, but increase your diminished self. If you are from a minority group it is worse. What do they do to diminish you?

Your natural rhythms of eating, drinking, urinating, defecating, and sleeping that were modified to fit your parents' schedule are now much more rigorously defined and enforced. Your body becomes increasingly alienated from itself. It is forced to respond to arbitrary schedules or be punished. If you are able to fit into the imposed schedules without physical discomfort or harm you are lucky. But, you can't escape the psychological damages.

First is the fact that you further lose your ability to recognize and read what your body is telling you. This causes physical illnesses to get out of hand because you are not aware of their early signs. You doubt your judgement about what you're experiencing so that doctors end up telling you what you're feeling. Is it any wonder so many people are misdiagnosed and mistreated?

Second is the psychological damage from your belief that what you feel and think is either invalid or not as important as what you are supposed to feel and think. You are supposed to go to the washroom at certain times and if you don't you are made to feel as if something is wrong with you.

In high school one teacher made the students wear a toilet seat around their head if they went to the toilet during class. Most teachers thought this was a clever idea because few students ever left his class. To me it said that the content of his class and his ego were more important than the self-respect of his students.

School is one-answer oriented. If you get the right answer you begin to feel that you are okay; if you didn't get it, you aren't OK. In real life there are many solutions to almost every situation or problem, yet your schools teach you to think in a narrow one-answer fashion.

School is supposed to teach you skills which will help you get a job, be a valuable citizen, pursue the ideals of democracy and lead a Christian life of brotherhood and love.

For the poor the idea of a job is hypocritical. Although enough of them can get out of the vicious cycle if they are truly exceptional intellectually or athletically, the vast majority cannot. Some of the poor will be the human machines still necessary for the running of a complex society (mainly service jobs). Most will be marginally supported by the state and spend their lives in poverty or crime.

For the majority in the schools from the lower middle and middle class, in their working lives they will be the masters of the poor, but they themselves will toil for bosses who have greater intelligence, power, and/or money. Those who control the board rooms of the country are those who went to private schools (inherited wealth) or those few who were able to overcome their public schooling and modest socio-economic background.

It is necessary in a complex society to have some chiefs. Public schools and the naive people who run them (administrators, teachers, class-ified staff) unknowingly are controllers who believe they are educators. They think they are preparing the students for freedom and maximizing their vocational and life choices, but the opposite is true.

A slave cannot teach about freedom. A slave cannot teach another how to make wise choices because he can make few of his own. A slave cannot teach another the love of learning when learning is based upon choices and he cannot make these choices. Nevertheless, a slave can control other slaves.

The Germans took the capos from the masses of those about to die and the capos were effective controllers of the others in the camps. This was a case of simple survival. School people are in a much different position because they can see that what they do seems to help the majority. They cannot see themselves as perpetuators of a cruel system for the many and of only a materially good life for the rest.

How can I say this? Because if those who run the schools really understood the learning process they would not agree to the curriculum, the crowded classrooms, and the lack of materials. Most importantly they would fight for greater freedom for the children and themselves. They don't react in these wholesome ways because their minds have been enslaved by those who have created their diminished selves.

Schools cannot teach about democracy because schools are not democratic structures. They can only teach about democracy as an abstract concept. Look at the student councils and governments. They seldom have any real power. But then look at the faculty councils, they seldom have any real power either. How can teachers or principals teach about democracy when they are operating from their diminished selves? They can't and don't.

Possibly the cruelest hoax of all is the hypocrisy surrounding the ideas of Christian brotherhood and love. The schools are one place where many students could be safe, could be warm, could be well fed, and could learn to like themselves and others. Competition, racism, and sexism keep this from happening. Testing could be done without diminishing individual self-esteem. Learning could be done so students were interested and motivated so that they could like and enjoy others as they learned to like themselves.

All over the country teachers are told not to shout at students, not to demean them, but then they are expected to force students into learning materials and styles which are incompatible with their unique brains. Teachers are taught control techniques which emphasize positive reinforcers rather than taught how to interact with the students and their learning. Students are stroked and apparently loved by people who are controlling rather than helping them become confident, independent learners.

The healthiest victims are those who rebel, but most are trapped. How can you be angry at, rebel against a person who genuinely believes she loves you? Even if she is suffocating you, she is doing it for your own good. Most students are seduced by love or pallid affection into doing what they are told rather than becoming clear, independent thinkers.

Two

Your Giant Self

You came into the world physically naked. According to many theorists you were also naked intellectually and spiritually. You were tabula rasa, a blank slate upon which the experiences of life would write and create a unique person.

Parents, teachers, ministers, and politicians have used this concept to justify their ideas of what is best for the children. In the process they convinced the children that what they felt and thought was invalid or unimportant unless it fit with the beliefs of the adults. They were brainwashed by them.

They were partly wrong. Although you came into the world physically naked, you were not a blank slate to be written upon. Nor were you an empty vessel into which any belief, philosophy, or ideology could be poured without any reaction from you.

They were partly correct. The power of socialization is enormous and to resist it takes knowledge and courage. It is seldom within the powers of the young to do so in any productive way. Much of the rebellion of adolescents in every industrialized country is an effort to find a group identity different from that which has been imposed upon them. Then, within this second context, each boy or girl seeks to establish his or her own individual identity. Unfortunately, this struggle usually takes forms that are against something rather than for something.

Gangs are a case in point. Each member is acting against what his national culture and ethnic subculture have imposed upon him. As a group the gang creates a subculture within a subculture. In their gang subculture members (or leaders) make the rules and develop the rituals -- different from society's rules and rituals -- and then see everything from the narrow self-interests of the closed system within which they operate. Within these confines they each try to find some individual uniqueness and meaning to their lives.

By understanding your mind, body, and spirit and the processes and behaviors people and institutions use to control your thoughts and actions, you will be able to create your giant self.

Notice that I am not underlining, highlighting, nor capitalizing any words for greater emphasis. You have to determine what you believe is important and memorable for you. This is one of the steps you will take in creating your giant self.

At the moment you were conceived, you were totally unique. There was never in the four million years of our species anyone with your exact combination of genes. From that moment on as you interacted with your maternal environment you grew increasingly unique. Why? Because even if you were an identical twin, the amount and quality of the nutrients you received were different. This meant that the genetic ccde that allegedly determined everything about you (such as size, body shape, and enzyme efficiency) were being modified by the uncertainties of your mother's diet, her emotions, and your capacities to absorb and best utilize the nutrients her body fed you. So, starting as a unique person, you continued to interact with your maternal environment and your uniqueness grew.

Your DNA code is usually thought of as a linear, a step-by step, one-directional biochemical progression. Some believe that even the reasons and time of your death are determined by this code. Insurance companies bet on the accuracy of this determinism. Yet, the DNA does not exist in isolation. It is dependent on constant feedback from the messenger RNA and the biochemical soup it lives in. In this chemical soup brought by the bloodstream are hormones, enzymes, minerals, amino acids, and countless other factors manufactured by your body or ingested into it. These factors can slightly to greatly modify or change your initial code. The amount of smoking your mother does is an example. For some it may make only slight changes, while with others it may produce catastrophic changes.

At birth you left the protections of the maternal environment, but were protected and nurtured by the parental, familial one. Your genetic code and its initial modifications due to your interactions within your maternal environment were now operating in an arena with greater dangers, but with more opportunities.

The people and social influences in your wider arena began to exert their powers to mold you the way they felt was best for you and for them. You had choices even then and these choices were your interactions which helped you continue to create your individual uniqueness. At first these were negative reactions like spitting out foods you didn't like, crying to get attention, and other ploys to get your own way. Your helplessness was used as a strength because you were a stranger in a strange land and no one spoke your language.

As you acquired language and social skills your choices grew, but so did the expectations of the others in your environment. Each person and institution had a vested interest in you and wanted you to meet his or its expectations. Those pressures were intense and often conflicted with the ones pushing you to be the someone your genetic abilities and interests directed you to be.

Most of the time you didn't compromise, you capitulated. You gave up. Society, your friends, and family forced you into behaviors and patterns which were ruled by your diminished self. Each helped to define, to invent who you are.

Now, by reading this book, you are asking for another chance, another opportunity to make choices so that you can create your own life the way that you want. A life that unleashes both your genetic potentials and your personal learning can now help you fulfill whatever it is you are capable of becoming. In short, you can now define and create your giant self.

The process of creating your giant self is a lifelong one in which you consciously, thoughtfully, and courageously carve out your own destiny. It is not easy, or everyone would have done it. It is worthwhile, because your life is almost always exciting, challenging, productive, and fun. The fun is in the process of achieving, of realizing the potentials you were given.

A child with Down's Syndrome was able to go to college because he refused to allow the genetic givens to determine his life. In the other direction, I trashed my genetics and, because of sheer laziness and refusal to endure the pain and boredom of training, I didn't make it to the Olympics.

Life gives you many, many chances. I have wasted many of them because at the time I didn't know what I am now sharing with you. I was always a very successful teacher, but I only gave fifty per cent. Because teaching was easy for me, I made the same mistake I'd made as an athlete. Why bother to put forth that extra effort when I could get by without enduring discomfort or pain? Now that I give one hundred per cent I am considered a great teacher. I can give this much because I have unleashed my giant self.

I will define your giant self as that portion of you which enables you to utilize and/or consciously modify your genetic givens, uses the best of what society has to offer you, resists the forces which would make you see only your diminished self, and interacts with others in ways which enhance and enrich the lives of all you touch while enabling you to be the best you can be.

Notice that I equally stress a sense of social obligation as well as the unleashing and expression of your individual talents and desires. If in the activation or expression of your giant self you use, abuse, or in any way intentionally limit or damage the lives of others or pollute our shared environments, then you are responding from your diminished self.

The person who reads books on how to ruthlessly ascend the corporate ladder, the famous artist who is an outstanding and unique talent yet is intolerant of others, and the renowned scientist who has only contempt for the ideas of others may be successful in the eyes of the world, but I see them socially functioning from their diminished selves.

I have never read of nor met any person who in all the areas of his life was able to consistently act from the basis of his giant self. It is an ideal, a model to use so a person can constantly measure himself against the best he could be. Like trying to live by the political and social ideals of the Constitution or the social, ethical, and moral ideals of the Bible, the giant self is a model which lends itself to bringing out the very best in each person.

Because it is an ideal, it is elusive and cannot be totally achieved. It isn't something to be attained, but rather is a lifelong process of becoming. It means becoming the best you can be physically, mentally, emotionally, socially, and spiritually. All these interact, but sometimes, while working hard to perfect or improve one area, one or more of the others suffer. Consequently, you are always somewhat off balance. Constantly asking yourself whether your acting from your giant self is part of your effort to regain balance.

Just as the ideal or metaphor of the giant self emphasizes your best, the metaphor of the diminished self is used to emphasize your failure to live up to the ideal of what could or should be. By understanding your diminished self, how it was created, how it is sustained, you will be able to recognize when you are functioning (or malfunctioning) within its confining and limiting structures.

In essence the giant self is all that you can be to best serve yourself and your world, while the diminished self is all that limits the expression of the best of you.

Of course, when a person writes a great book, discovers a cure for some disease, overcomes any kind of handicap, or does anything that others would have liked to accomplish, it is seen as an expression of his giant self. However, I see it as being expressed in countless small ways as well. The child who steps up to the plate who possesses very little athletic skill, the woman who timidly stands up to a bullying parent or spouse, the sales clerk who sees a better way to organize the clothing, or the smoker who considers others by altering his behavior are examples of ways a person can express his giant self.

Any activity that shows the person is breaking away from a previously induced program, that allows him to realize more of his genetic or acquired potentials and skills is an expression of his giant self. Aware that he is eating too much fat and changing his diet, understanding how meditation can increase his spirituality and beginning to practice it, or recognizing the depth of his prejudice and confronting it through psychotherapy, reading, or involvement are evidence of the giant self.

Three

Your Diminished Self

How was your diminished self created? By others, by your society, and by the realities of your own human vulnerability.

Realistically, your powers are limited. When you were born and for many years after you were largely dependent upon your parents to meet all your basic human needs. If you were to get your needs met you learned their language, belief systems, and what was expected of you. You may have acted rebellious when you didn't get what you wanted, but you didn't challenge their language or belief systems.

Although a baby and very young child sees the world egocentrically, he is aware that everyone around him is larger and more capable. When my granddaughter says, "You got to help me Papa, my little fingers is too small," she is expressing her awareness of her limited powers. It is a healthy request by her because she feels that it is a temporary thing. She knows she will get bigger and be more competent. She doesn't feel diminished, just realistically limited.

However, if I teased her or became irritated by her request, then I would be giving her the message that she was incompetent and a burden. This is a message creating a diminished self. If my daughter, wife, or I only occasionally put her off, however, her self-image and self-confidence would not be seriously damaged.

What I see as a teacher are children whose parents often take their temporary inabilities to perform certain tasks and magnify that into proof of a permanent incompetency. The child finally believes he cannot do anything right and gradually stops trying and becomes dependent on others to do his thinking. He has been trained to believe that his diminished self is him.

A temporary lack of development of a skill at a certain time, or a lack of proper training and understanding by the parent has created within the child an attitude and belief in his incompetence, which is perpetuated.

Shel, my granddaughter, had three bad experiences in various swimming pools before she was three. This could have left her permanently afraid and a non-swimmer. My wife slowly built on Shel's

24

trust in her and moved her from the jacuzzi to arm floats and then to becoming a competent, fearless swimmer before she was four. Marie stayed with her, eased her into each step as she gained more competence and confidence. She built on Shel's giant self and each time her diminished self would surface, Marie would remind her how much she had learned and how competent she was. She would observe her closely and gently challenge her to take the next step.

At four she dives and swims everywhere in the pool. This did not just happen. A loving, thoughtful adult took the time to closely observe when the child was ready to be eased into the next level of development.

This is the exception. The adults are busy with their own concerns and the child's temporary incompetencies or developmental differences become proof to the child that he is stupid or worthless. If your own experience was typical, every error, mistake, or poor judgement was seen by your parents as evidence of your incompetency. You shared their belief.

A child needs to understand that he is not expected to be a miniature-sized adult. He needs to know that he is a complicated being who is growing at different rates than others his same age and sex. Therefore, he should be compared only with himself. Usually, if allowed to grow at his own rate and not judged and put down, he will catch up or at least achieve at his competency levels.

I did terrible damage to my daughter, Lisa, because I wanted her to be everything I wasn't. I pushed her, was impatient, and although she was an extraordinary child, nothing she did was ever quite good enough. This was an attitude my dad had towards me and I had thought I would never impose upon my children.

The positive side of it was she was a straight A student in college and graduate school. Her desire to be perfect drives her to scrupulously plan for each of the children in her class. She is an outstanding teacher, but still carries within her my earlier, demanding attitude.

You, like Lisa, like me, have imprinted in your brain, many of the negative comments, the disgusted and disappointed looks, and the actions of your parents which created your diminished self before your giant self had a chance to develop and emerge.

Even if your parents had been totally supportive and encouraged your gradual development, the limitations of your senses, body, and brain would have made you doubt what you saw and felt. I'll explain this in a later chapter, but the point is that being human, you make mistakes based on faulty sensory data. Even if others excuse these errors, you know they are considered mistakes, and these help impede your giant self and convince you that your diminished self is the real you.

And then you enter the schools. If a group got together and planned the most diabolic way to destroy a child's emerging giant self, they'd have a hard time being more destructive than any school system in the world.

Crowded together in rooms that were designed by men more interested in factory-like efficiency than in human comfort, forced to follow a curriculum designed by people who seemed to have little knowledge of individual or developmental differences, run by people operating from their own diminished selves who find comfort in pettiness, schooling is a moment by moment diminishment of the best in humans.

Why this terrible accusation when schools have done so much for modern man? Because they can easily do much better. As schools operate now, every child and adult experiences many types of failure each day.

I am considered a superior teacher, yet I say and do things I shouldn't, or don't say or do things that I should, which harms my students. When I do this I am acting from my diminished self.

Remember an average day in school. If you were the bright one, you had to be anxious lest you made an error. You were under constant pressure and often, because of jealousy, you were disliked by many of your peers. If you were average, you were always being nagged to do better. You had to work hard, but you knew you could never be anything great because most of the things you were interested in and valued were not important in school. You learned to live with your mediocrity by joining in with others as they preyed upon one another. Favorite prey were those who were either physically unattractive, poorer than you, or mentally slow. If you were in one of those groups your life was a constant, living hell.

Parent conferences were the times when home and school reinforced their mutual mistaken beliefs about you and accentuated your diminished self.

When you began working, you started at the bottom. This meant that you had little power over your life. If you were fortunate you had a boss who knew what he was doing and who treated you well. For the average person work was like school. It was a constant battle to keep from being put down by peers or your superiors. Because of your diminished self and its negative power, you were afraid to try something new, or, if you did, you brought your loser mentality to it so the same problems recurred.

If you found someone to love you, your partner probably was mostly functioning at his/her diminished self level. Love is blind. This means that hormone secretions are so powerful that for awhile a sow's ear looks like a silk purse. However, as the assaults on the ego by others build up, the diminished self dominates the relationship. Soon you are no longer building on one another's giant self, but picking, pettily, jealously upon the diminished self of your partner.

Love, which is the opportunity to break the cycle, cannot survive what the other is experiencing in his social and work life and so the destructive cycle is continued.

It doesn't take tragedies like losing a job, or being divorced to be diminished. This can happen as the result of constant little erosions of your self and sense of self-worth.

When you're waiting in line and the clerk seems not to notice you. You feel invisible, a non entity. When you're driving in your car and some little kid sticks his tongue out at you or gives you the finger. It's trivial, but it makes you wonder, why me? Your parent or spouse says or does something that he knows bothers you, you've asked him not do it, but he does it and makes it worse by laughing.

I will be offering explanations of why I think people do these things to each other, but at this time I merely want you to understand why your diminished self is more dominant than your giant self and how it is maintained.

I can usually recognize when my diminished self is in charge. I feel out of control. I make errors in speaking, am more physically clumsy, and say things that hurt others. These are times I wish my life had an instant replay button with which I could undo my mistake and then relive the event more in keeping with my giant self.

Suggestion: You can do this by the simple expedient of a sincere apology given as soon after the event as you can muster the courage to admit you have made a mistake. I have found that the sooner I do this the easier it is, the least amount of damage occurs, and no matter what the other person does, I feel terrific.

When I'm operating within my giant self, the pettiness of others rolls off me easier. I understand they are under the influence of their diminished selves and, by taking that into account, I can be more generous, take their remarks less personally, or be up front and confrontive to them, but in an understanding or humorous manner.

Actually, the more I feel I am in my giant self mode, I appear more confident, am more friendly and tolerant, and I am seldom assaulted by others' diminished selves.

So, you have a giant self that encompasses all that you are and can be through effort, thought, and luck and that is constantly under attack by the diminished selves of those you meet as well as by your own diminished self. Your diminished self is reinforced more often than is your giant self. However, by understanding what causes or creates each self, you can consciously place yourself in your giant self mode. It takes thought, courage, and practice, but with effort your life can improve radically for the better, though not if it's based on unrealistic expectations.

Four

Unfulfilled Unrealistic Expectations

Each person has what Dr. Stanley Krippner calls, a "personal myth." Krippner's formulation deals mostly with dreams, but it fits here. Your personal myth is the picture you carry in your mind about who you are. It is a myth because of the differences between who you think you are and the realities of your life. The reality is often too painful, belittling, or frightening to face in its totality so you change the truth to fit this personal myth which you can live with.

In any intimate relationship you bring your myth. Therefore, you start the relationship with some aspects of yourself that are hidden from your partner, and yourself. I am not speaking about the things which you are purposely hiding to make a good impression, but those that are hidden unconsciously. These myths will cause unrealistic expectations which cannot be fulfilled. These expectations cannot be met because they are based on the myths and false premises you, and then, your partner share. You are unconsciously falsifying who you are and you believe you will understand him and he you, but since your myth is based on errors or lies, I contend that neither of you can truly understand the other.

Some people are physiologically more energetic in the day, others at night. Suppose you are a night person (NP) in a relationship with a day person (DP). Myths will cause disappointments. When the DP begins to run down, wants to rest, or sleep, you are getting into high gear. He may have forced himself to be highly energetic at night in the beginning of the relationship, but can no longer sustain the myth, because he would get run-down and ill.

In order to impress you he played a role which he could sustain temporarily because the initial excitement of a new relationship was so stimulating that he could overcome his physical tendencies.

You may have done the same. Possibly in the morning you are like an attack dog until you have your coffee or a time to adjust to the obtrusive daylight. To pacify him you talked sweetly, maybe even smiled at his morning exuberance, while secretly harboring murderous thoughts.

Neither of you can continue your myths because they go against your physiology. If you had been honest in the beginning of your relationship, you could have worked more easily towards a compromise, but you would have risked losing the other. Very few people are willing to risk losing someone if there is a strong sexual, financial or any other beneficial attraction.

So, most people weave myths about themselves, as well as go along with the myths of the other, because they have little faith in their giant selves. The myth, no matter how grandiose it appears, is built upon the shaky diminished self. The movie, "Cross My Heart," is an example of two people beginning a relationship based on what they thought the other wanted from him/her. They consciously lied. This is different from your personal myth, which is usually unknown to you. However, the lies can become part of the myth and gradually, through rationalization, also be hidden from you.

Especially in the beginning of a relationship, your efforts to impress the other make you susceptible to your own and the other's personal myths.

The DP is afraid to admit he is tired or not able to function well in a night setting because you might get angry and drop him. He can't admit his tiredness, even thought it is normal, because it may be seen by you as weakness. He must try to meet your expectations, even thought they do not fit him. He forces himself to stay awake, pretends to have a good time, and then, just as stupidly, he is secretly angry at you.

This anger confuses him because he agreed to live up to your expectations, but physiologically he can't do this as often or continuously as you can. Since he is dishonest about his real feelings, he is puzzled why he says or does something hostile to you. He's been trained to reject or ignore his real feelings and so he operates on his personal myth which is his "supposed-to-be-real" self.

In turn you are hurt and/or hostile because you have assumed he is enjoying the night, as you are. You are upset because his anger or hostility seems to be without foundation and so you can't understand his reactions.

Suppose one of you has allergies. Alan wants to share his strawberries with you, his fair lady. He has never had a runny nose, burning eyes, the closing of the throat, or the rash you experience when eating them. He may press you to try them again; he may talk about how allergies are all in your head; or he may eat them in front of you while belittling your mental and emotional weakness.

Strawberries are known to be allergenic, but what if your allergy is to a food not known for its allergenic nature, or to a place, or a smell? Your partner, or any non allergic person, tends not to believe or understand your suffering. There is no common ground of experience, so you cannot explain your discomfort and misery. The other person remains unsympathetic because your allergy interferes with the relationship. Your allergy is real, but he sees it as an irritant or inconvenience to him. He has unrealistic expectations which you cannot meet.

What if your partner has an addiction? I don't expect you to begin a relationship with a person who has a serious substance abuse problem. If you have, it isn't just unrealistic, it is self-destructive. It also is a sad demonstration of a person totally dominated by his/her diminished self. I am referring to minor addictions to things like chocolate, coffee, tea, or any food or drink. If you don't share the obsession, it's likely you will look upon it as a weakness in the other's character. If it bothers you and you initially put up with it with plans that later, when your relationship is more secure, you will change it, you are suffering from unrealistic expectations which will remain unfulfilled. If he does curtail or control his addiction, just for you, you can be certain you will be paying an emotional price you'll regret.

Left-handers were considered possessed by the devil and until the past few decades most parents tried to make their LH children RH before they got to school. The world is basically constructed for the convenience of right-handers. If your partner is LH you may get irritated because he does not do some things as you think they should be done. He experiences differently even the minor things in life, like opening a door, buttering toast, or tying his shoes. He actually sees and feels many events from a different perspective. I am not saying his or your way is better, only different, but you may be sending a value-laden message. He may interpret it, correctly, as meaning that you see him in a diminished manner. If you laugh or put down his perspective, you create problems with his diminished self that will damage your relationship. Both of you actually see the events somewhat differently. If you shared your perceptions instead of judging each other, you could bridge the gap between the differences perceived.

Intelligence is a complex entity with many facets and dimensions. There is intelligence that comes from formal education and that which develops from the experiences of living. There is intelligence using the scientific method/logic mode and that of the intuitive/feeling mode. All are legitimate ways of knowing, and of error, but in our society intuition is associated with women and not considered as valid by many men. A woman voicing her intuitive feelings may be put down by her man because he believes she is not being logical. They are operating on two different ways of using intelligence and dealing with reality, but each believes his or hers is more valid. Neither is willing to fulfill the other's expectations.

In teaching hundreds of people to use visualization to solve problems I have been amazed at the differences in their imaging abilities in the various senses. Some people cannot see colors or shapes. Some cannot hear anything but my voice while others clearly hear entire musical scores or sounds in a forest. Some salivate at the sumptuous dinner I invoke while others may see it; and some others get a sense of it, but cannot smell, taste, or see it. If your partner gets orgasmic about a taste and you don't get the same intensity, he will be disappointed and from within his diminished self he may verbally attack you.

The above examples are based on physiological differences that people are aware of, but don't consider serious enough to be a basis for misunderstandings. All are expectations on the part of one person which the other cannot fulfill. Besides the unfulfillable physiological expectations, there are those that stem from social or psychological factors that are the result of past experiences, differences in cultures, and combinations of these.

Emotional communication is a multiple problem There is a body of research which indicates that men and women do not conceptualize the meanings in communications in the same manner. Men, whether because of their rearing or brain levels of serotonin and body levels of testosterone, communicate from a position of aggressively controlling the conversation and their feelings. Women, whose blood levels of estrogen and progesterone, affect their feelings, want the conversation to reflect an expression of their emotions as well as the intellect/logic mode with which men are more comfortable.

Therapeutically, dealing with most couples is like watching two different species or cultures trying to communicate. Women and men truly see and experience the world differently. It is a combination of physiological differences beyond the obvious large plumbing ones. If an ingestion of a miniscule amount of LSD can cause gross changes, what do major amounts of female and male hormones do to the way men and women view the world? It seems obvious that they will each judge their experiences from their own inner worlds. Each will unrealistically expect the other to see and feel the same way about an event because it is what he or she is experiencing. It is a no-win scenario.

The impact of the amounts of hormonal difference is obvious with transsexuals. They claim they lived their lives (before their operations) trapped in the body of the wrong sex. Besides the tissue additions or subtractions, they have to have hormone therapy to help them more clearly be one sex. Without the hormone treatment the transition is not as complete.

Everyone has the hormones of both sexes, but the genetic instructions give each the proper amounts to make him or her clearly one sex. Because the body is so complex, minor errors are common and sometimes the directions are not strong enough in one direction. This can result in confusion regarding sexual identity. The hormone therapy helps the transsexual more comfortably feel like his chosen sex. Of course, he can also actually feel his new sex which must be a pleasant reinforcement.

With the average couple their sexual identities are very specific and different enough so that it is difficult for each to appreciate what the other is experiencing. In mediating conflicts I attempt to get each to see and explain how he and she are experiencing the same situation. Both claim they are communicating. Instead, each is propagandizing, pleading, and trying to influence the other to accept his or her point-of-view. They speak of communication, but what they are seeking is validation, agreement. (Despite my training and experience, my wife and I still get trapped in these diminished self positions which are not discussions or communications, but self-protective measures.)

I try to teach couples to appreciate the real differences between them and to admit how difficult it is to get into the other's reality. I have to teach them to listen to the other and turn off their hormonally determined sexual differences and see their common humanness.

Others are trapped in a slimy sea of bad past experiences with others, often of the opposite sex, so they slide into this sea at the slightest perceived attack by the other. They are victims of unfinished business from their childhood which distorted their primary male/female relationships and now it becomes one of the main reasons why they have expectations which cannot be realistically fulfilled. Or, they have negative expectations and they unconsciously set up the situations so that they will be disappointed.

Example: If a woman has seen her father and step-fathers constantly emotionally belittle her mother she will expect that type of treatment from the men in her life. Either she will select men that do so or she will set up situations in which only a saint wouldn't abuse her. She does not do this on purpose, but her expectations and experiences need to be fulfilled in ways she is familiar with, even though they are painful and destructive.

What can you do? Are happy, fulfilling relationships ever possible? Yes. Individual, family, and group counseling is one answer. Classes such as I give in Stress Management provide information about relationships and afford one the opportunity to discuss the real differences between the sexes in a rational, protective setting.

However, there are no simple answers and therapy isn't effective for everyone. Furthermore, the problems within any human relationship are as enduring as is the relationship. As much as you grow to love and understand the other person, you still want your own way. And so does the other person. If you can be honest about this, it clears away much of the garbage and deceit. Then, by recognizing the enormous differences between you, each begins a lifelong process of clearly and honestly making her needs known while listening carefully to what the other wants.

Don't try to read minds. If one of you is certain she knows what the other is going to say, then she's probably wrong and is not allowing the other to speak his mind. You cannot fulfill yours or the other's expectations until you know what they are. At that point you can accept, reject, or negotiate. In fact, visualize yourselves as two negotiators. Each represents a powerful government which is seeking peace, not war. You want to get all you can for your country, but you know that other negotiator has to be equally successful or his people will fire or kill him.

Therefore, you must understand his history, his experiences, his fears, loves, ideals, and exactly what he needs to consider himself successful. He must treat you with the same respect. Then, together, you forge a compromise which is livable for each.

If, from your perspective, you have given in and didn't get what you feel you need or deserve, or he feels that way, then the one who feels most cheated will have such underlying frustration and anger that he will undermine the compromise.

Each of you needs to see that your relationship will be an endless series of negotiations, barterings, and compromises in which sometimes one gets a little more, but in the long haul both derive much from it. The more honest you are, the easier it will be to deal with your differences and the compromises will increasingly be mutually satisfying.

It is hardly a perfect solution, but then I said that with every solution a new problem arises. I reiterate the certainty of uncertainty.

You need to learn to live with a constant degree of insecurity. This is reality.

I offer you a process, not a solution. The process allows you to learn to be understanding of your physiological differences which create psycho-sociological differences. You need to express your needs in a way that is nourishing, nurturing, logical, and loving so that your expectations are reasonable and can be fulfilled.

Five

Personal Myth:
Memories of a Past That Never Was

I hitchhiked on Krippner's use of personal myth in dreams and transformed it into your personal memories of the past. Carl Jung, in his autobiography, also states that it is impossible to accurately remember your past. What you do is recreate it in ways that can be called myth-making. A myth is a story or an explanation of some practice, belief, institution, or natural phenomenon which is allegedly based on some real, but forgotten historical data. It can also be based on remembrances that are much more fictional than factual. The way they are remembered serves unconscious and conscious emotional purposes. Myths can be emotionally satisfying metaphors which you use to explain past behavior.

Even if you didn't have emotional or other reasons for not remembering your past accurately, there are the normal physiological limitations in the accuracy of anyone's memories.

If twenty people of the same sex, culture, general intelligence, and interest observe and experience the same event at the same time, their reports, verbal and written will be idiosyncratic. Each will process the event differently.

Research on memory has consistently demonstrated that 80-90 per cent of what is learned is forgotten within twenty-four hours, unless it is reinforced or seen as very important. Past experience with the data makes the retention higher, because the person has a structure to build upon. The motivation or degree of interest further adds to or subtracts from the amount retained.

The number and intensity of the brain subsections and sense modalities involved will also determine how much and how accurately the event is recalled.

Finally, how an event fits in with your present personal myth will make a pronounced difference. If you see yourself as an independent person and the event seems to prove otherwise, you will selectively remember mostly those parts which support your personal myth.

Where did your concept of you originate and develop? Before you were born many people, including your parents, had some very specific conceptions of who you were going to be. These expectations would later help define you. However, at the moment of conception, the genetic dice spun in a tiny chemical pool and the individual you was somewhat determined. I say somewhat because the interaction with your maternal environment would modify you. During these two major influences choice and intentionality on your part were absent. (Some evidence from physics and biology may prove there is choice and some rudimentary consciousness from the moment of conception on.)

After birth your interactions with the adults in your external environment were still limited by your dependency, your genetic givens, and the behavior of these adults. The way they treated you was largely determined by factors beyond your control, one of which was their original expectations about you. Your choices and your controls over your life were limited to acting upon body instructions such as hunger, tiredness, and need for warmth and reacting to events initiated by those in your environment.

From the beginning there was no clear-cut "you" that was not either physically a part of some others such as parents and grandparents or that wasn't being defined by them into their conception of you.

Example: My mother wanted a loving, passive boy who was a good student. Her conception made it easy for me to give her an innocent look and a plaintive sigh and she chose to believe my lies. As a pre-teen I was the leader of a gang of thieves that sneaked into theaters, stole from stores, and never got caught. She had plenty of evidence because I had mountains of books, comic books, games, and school supplies that I could never have bought from the tiny allowance I was given.

I rebelled against her conception of me that I saw as a goody two-shoes image. Yet, I was very well-mannered and courteous, especially to adults, so she had managed to shape a part of me to her expectations.

My father wanted a boy who was aggressive and powerful. When I used to flit around the living room, dancing to classical music his mind flashed a neon light screaming queer, queer, queer. So, although I had the natural grace and rhythm to be a ballet dancer, which I wanted to be, his looks froze out ballet as a means of expression or a career. Instead, he taught me to box by knocking me all around the living room. This helped in creating the liar and thief and made me mean and vicious. Coupled with my genetic givens, this training made me a very successful competitive athlete and sadistic boxer. He had defined a part of me and shaped me to his expectations.

My paternal grandmother, who died when I was seven, wanted me to be a religious boy who loved God. I remember the security and love I felt in the synagogue while sitting between her and my grandfather. I felt safe, happy, and believed God loved me and all the other Jews. Her early training shaped me into her expectations. If she hadn't died and had continued her enormous influence I probably would have become a rabbi.

These people had expectations very different, but each shaped my life. With each, like a chameleon or kaleidoscope, I was the colors, the person, of their expectations.

Who was I, where was the real me? I was all of them. Is it any wonder man is such a confused, complex being? Each of us is a composite of the definitions and expectations of each of the major people in our lives. We are proportionately affected by every other minor figure who we need, or needs us, or uses or is used by us.

As I was, you were totally dependent on your parents or parent substitutes to meet all your needs. As you grew older your interactions with these and other significant adults began to fall into predictable patterns of behavior. These patterns of behavior are what people referred to when they spoke of you. Even as an adult that is true. People judge who you are by what you do. The first thing people want to know when they meet you is what you do. If you're a doctor, teacher, waitress, or unemployed, they believe that they know you by what you do. What they can tell is part of your patterns of behavior because each job demands specific behaviors that are generally known from the title. (In the early Sixties, after my divorce, I lived with a female teacher. A few other couples had the same kind of living arrangement. Under the rules in the LA District any of us could have been fired for moral turpitude. We easily got away with it because no one believed that teachers could act so unconventionally; i.e., we didn't fit into their patterns of teacher behavior.)

As a child these predictable patterns were referred to as your personality. Although these patterns were strong, they were affected by the expectations of the person with whom you interacted. There was not a pure you which could not be modified depending on the power of the person you were interacting with. You were never an entity isolated from others and your identity was a meshing of the generalized you plus the specific patterns expected by the other person.

In school, in church, and other public arenas the same thing happened and the kaleidoscopic "you" grew in complexity and the patterns increased. This kaleidoscope, this you that reacts somewhat differently to each person you meet would be totally unpredictable and a chaotic mess, if some of the patterns didn't predominate. You try on these patterns, these behaviors in your reactions to different people. You find that some patterns are more effective and you use them more frequently because they work.

Example: Almost everyone learns that those with more power like to be stroked by addressing them with their titles or treating them with the deference they feel they've earned. I will respond more favorably to a student who refers to me as "Dr. Rose," than to those who call me, "Mr. Rose," and least favorably to those who want to call me, "Bob." I recognize that each tells me something about the student and gives me clues on how to approach him.

I make no bones about the fact I like the prestige of my doctorates and "Dr. Rose" is how I want them to address me. At the same time I give them exactly the same respect in that I will address them with the title, name, or nickname that they want.

I am predictable. I have a pattern of behavior that shows some consistency. This makes it easier for those who work with me to understand my behavior. If, during class, some child addresses me as, "Bob," the others know I will follow certain predictable behaviors. I will gently remind the child that I earned my degrees and I would appreciate being called "Dr. Rose." If the child persists, I will tell him I respect and call him by the name he requested and I expect the same thoughtfulness. If he still persists I will ask him why he is treating me in a way that I don't like. The next step is punishment. These are predictable because I use them over and over and over in the same general circumstances.

What I refer to as me, and you refer to as you, are these general patterns we use to cope with the different people we meet. Your kaleidoscopic self has within it a rich display of general patterns which you use depending on your reading of the person with whom you're interacting. As long as a pattern gives you the results you want you keep using it. If it isn't working you try other patterns until you find one that works.

Unfortunately, with some people and situations none of your patterns work. If you're able to generate new one's and they still don't work, your behavior gets increasingly disorganized. The patterns break down. You become "crazy," sick, or, in frustration, you repeat one pattern despite its ineffectiveness.

However, most of the time for most people, the patterns become routine, ingrained, and recognizable as you. The people, events, and time sequence of these patterns are what I refer to as the historical you. If a continuous movie could be made of you from the moment of conception this would be the historical you. If the movie could be made in such a way that there were no value judgements made, it would be a statement of the historical you. This is impossible. There is only the kaleidoscopic you -- a you that is totally mixed up in value judgements, fears, ignorance, pettiness, prejudice, and filled with insecurities.

Discouraging? These are some of the drawbacks of being human and having an astonishingly complex and rich brain. It is a brain that takes these patterns, these people and institutions you have interacted with and constantly creates a montage of the past. This montage, very loosely based on the historical self, paints pictures of the past that fit with whatever are your present and believed future needs, as well as selections from the past. They may be flattering or not. They may be partially or not at all in synch with what happened historically. These memories and responses are always defined by the person or persons you are with. This historical you is plastic or shapeable by what you believe are the expectations of the other person(s). This historical you is like a main dish and the expectations of others are like spices that change your flavor depending on their strength and quality.

It happens subtly. My ex-father-in-law wanted to dominate me, but I successfully resisted. After four years in the Air Force I thought he had little control over my wife or me. So, when we moved back to LA, I would pacify him to make my wife happy. One day I woke up and realized I was living my life according to his expectations. It took me years to break away from the "me" as he saw and created it.

What makes you remember certain things, forget others? You remember best the things that are most important to you. You generally distort situations in which you look bad. But, if you're operating from your diminished self, you will unconsciously change events to fit into your diminished self pattern. If you cannot face a situation in which you behaved badly, judged by others' evaluation of it, you will reconstruct it to fit the way you want to see it.

Your personal myth is all the patterns you develop to explain your past. Since life is insecure, uncertain, filled with ambiguities and paradoxes, your personal myth has a certain fluidity to it to fit the person or situation.

Personal myths can be educational, beautiful or ugly, uplifting or degrading, but always revealing of the deeper texture of your being.

Despite a reputation (given to me by whom? friends, relatives, enemies, myself?) as a boxer, football player, and mean dude, I hated confrontations that were verbally loud. My personal myth was tied to being an effective fighter because I had proven my toughness in the past so, I could avoid any fights and still be considered a tough guy.

Another choice, and a reason not to fight, was I could run for help since I had been a sprint champion. My wife didn't find my logical concept of running for help funny nor was she consoled by my statements that I was just being honest since most people would prefer flight to fight. She hated my talking about this kind of situation and when even my dreams reflected this cowardly pattern she got very angry.

Finally, one day she exploded and said she didn't want a rational man, but a husband who she could rely on to protect her and our children. The depth of her fears and her disappointment in me were communicated so forcefully that I was shaken.

I realized that I was allowing logic and my real fears to dominate my thinking. I said I was sorry and I promised that I would not let her down in an emergency. A few nights later I had a dream in which we were in danger. Despite my fears I acted bravely and saved her. I was exhilarated. I shared it with Marie. She was dubious, but subsequent similar type dreams convinced her. Since then, with very few exceptions, my dreams reflected my courage in the face of personal pain, danger, or death as I saved her or the children.

A personal myth had formalized a pattern of cowardice which I had neatly rationalized. By being forced to recognize its damaging characteristics I was able to consciously create my future responses by reconstructing my past. By formalizing the new pattern, which expressed itself first in my dreams and which required a stance I had seen as silly and illogical, I had programmed myself to think of acting in a way that made Marie feel protected.

In recent years when there have been serious earthquakes that posed possible dangers, I have leaped from bed and moved to warn or save Marie or our children. When there were possible intruders, even though I was not always convinced of the danger, I investigated out of respect for Marie's fears. Before, I would have said let them take what they want, it was not worth the risk. I believed that this was based on my experiences as a probation officer and my knowledge of the unpredictability of criminals. However, I changed my personal myth of my possible cowardice, which I explained as logical behavior, because I realized I was not dealing with Marie's logic, but her deeper, more primitive fears. Because I love her I was able to see how my myth affected her and I consciously changed it.

One of my high school friends still tells people stories of how everywhere we went others would defer to me and no one would dare mess with our group. He saw me bloody a few guys in the ring, but never saw me in a street fight. Yet his myth about me, as well as others', made me believe the same thing. Because of it, I was so cocky at seventeen that I fought a guy almost fifty pounds heavier, three inches taller, and seven years older. In about eight minutes he thoroughly destroyed my personal myth as well as an army of brain cells.

This is the way many of our personal myths are shattered. In some cases what is called mental illness is the disintegration of many long-term and cherished personal myths. When the person reconstructs his life on the basis of his real feelings and abilities rather than memories of a past that never was, then he has his life based on a more firm foundation.

Teacher after teacher had shaped me by telling me how smart I was and how easily I learned things. This developed into the myth that I could or should learn effortlessly. It worked up until graduate school. At that point the competition was so great, and the classes necessitated so much more effort and thought, that I was unable to pass some of my comprehensive exams. I absolutely would not read a chapter or textbook twice because it was an admission that I was not as smart as my myth asserted. It was an unproductive collusion between my personal myth as defined by others and my diminished self.

Now, I'll read something until it makes sense or I'll even ask someone else what it means. I am no longer run by that myth of intellectual infallibility, but by my giant self which tells me that I don't have to know everything, I don't have to get the meaning the first time, nor do I have to learn complicated ideas quickly. If I had been freed from this myth in my teens or at least during college, I would probably have become the child psychiatrist I wanted to be.

What can you do about your personal myths? Remember that they are loosely based on the historical you, but even that was shaped by what others did and said to you. If your mother constantly used the word stupid while referring to you and your behavior, it would have been impossible for you not to have incorporated that into your mythic self. And, that would have to be a myth because you couldn't have read this far and be stupid. Others probably have tried to tell you that you were not stupid, but your mother's words are physiologically as well as psychologically imbedded in the electrochemical environments of your brain. They are there for life. They cannot be eradicated except by surgery, but no surgeon would know what to remove since every memory is a combination, a synthesis of various parts of the brain. Since you cannot destroy it physically or mentally, you must supplant it by a stronger idea.

By reading this book you are attempting to recreate yourself. Your original self was developed from your genetic givens, the people whom you depended upon, your interactions with these factors, plus elements of conscious choice.

Through heightening your awareness, your consciousness of who said and did what to you, you can understand the persons, events, and institutions which shaped you. Now, as a thinking person you can intentionally select and choose how to shape the rest of your life. If you continue to make choices based on your diminished self, the one mainly defined by what others negatively thought about you, then you will have no one to blame. If you choose to make choices based on your abilities, strengths, and the best of yourself, then more of your life will reflect your giant self.

The more choices made from your giant self, the more you will distance yourself form the handicaps and limitations imposed upon you by your personal myth and diminished self. The old myths will always pop up, usually when you're in a weakened state mentally, physically, or emotionally. It's similar to the ease with which you contract illness when your immune system is weak. When you're weak, these old myths will reappear. However, like an alcoholic who knows he is always susceptible to liquor, you must keep in mind that all the bad things you believed about yourself are still very much alive within your brain.

It is your giant self that brings out your best which must intentionally, consciously, and often through personal courage, utilize your strengths and not succumb to fears and old responses. You need not continue old or build new negative personal myths, because you are the architect of your giant self.

Six

Unfinished Business:
Hauntings and Hurrahs

The clerk sneers and says, "Isn't it obvious how that works? The button clearly states power. Without power it won't do much."

The man deserves an equally deflating reply or an immediate trip to an emergency room, but you say nothing. You feel the way you did countless times before when your mother spoke to you in the same derogatory tone. You stand there helpless and probably apologize for being so stupid. Of course, you should have been more observant, but the clerk's job is to make your understanding of the workings of the machine easier. He is being lazy and his tone is unnecessary.

If you were able to operate on the basis of your giant self, you could handle it this way: "I'm asking you questions because I have not read the directions. I'm depending on your expertise to save my time and assure me I won't use it improperly. I have not done anything to hurt you and I don't deserve, nor will I tolerate being treated rudely. Now, can we get on with my questions?"

At no time was I rude, but I was in control. I was not allowing him to manipulate me. In your case your unfinished business with your mother prevented you from doing what you wanted to and should have done. Unfinished business means being locked into a pattern of behavior with one person which you inappropriately transfer to situations that feel similar. You further reinforce this habitual pattern which will make it easier for you to be diminished by the person who originated your problem and every subsequent person who makes you feel the same way.

There are two ways of handling this. The best is to confront the originator of the pattern -- if you know. One of the purposes of some types of therapy is to find out who created these patterns, imprints, or programs which run your life. For example suppose it is your mother. She is the one who controls this instance of unfinished business. Each time she belittles you and makes you feel stupid, you need to stop and confront her with it at the moment you begin to feel stupid.

44

Suppose you're visiting and helping her with the dishes. You start to place a cup in the cabinet and she lashes out with, "That doesn't go there! Why would I put cups up there and saucers in the left shelf?"

"Mom, I'm here because I love you and want to help you, but when you yell at me, I don't feel loved. You make me feel stupid."

"It's because you are stupid. Anyone who would put cups with —— "

"The issue is not cups, it's an attitude. If it wasn't cups, it would be something else. It's about how you have always treated me."

"I've always loved you. It's just that you don't think before you do things."

"Untrue. I've always thought, but since my thoughts didn't coincide with yours you assumed I was always wrong. I wasn't and I'm not. We don't have to agree or do things the same way to love one another. Dr. Rose says that if I'm ever going to become my giant self I have to explain my feelings to you and stand up for myself."

"Good for you. Now tell Dr. Rose to put the cups where they belong."

Chances are that when you finally confront such persons they will feel attacked and defensive. After all, you have been acting in a very predictable pattern for many years. Suddenly, you are wresting your share of power from them. They will be surprised, possibly quite angry, but it is the fear of their reaction that has been controlling you. You have to decide whether or not you are willing to risk their anger or withdrawal. In most cases people aren't willing to take these risks and their unfinished business lasts a lifetime.

One client spoke of a mother who constantly told her she was ugly and that no man would ever want her. She ended up being the only family member who stayed with her mother and cared for her until she (the client) was in her thirties. The first man who paid any attention to her, she married. He continued where the mother left off and she allowed him to sexually and emotionally abuse her.

During the session in which she finally realized how he controlled her in almost the same debasing way her mother had done, she became almost hysterical. Her mother and husband were dead and she was a sixty-five year old woman who felt her life had been a terrible waste. She worked through her anger as I helped her see how her tormentors had been miserable and tortured people too.

Through the process of guided imagery I had her relive various encounters with each. First I had her recall them as accurately as possible and feel her pain. Then, I would have her relive it again, but this time reconstruct it the way she wished she had responded.

Of course, it's much easier during imagery and she didn't have to courageously face either of them. However, since they were dead, short of seance, there was no way for her to confront them, except in this way. The important thing was that she broke her former patterns, created a giant self with her new pattern, and then applied it in her daily life.

In her last session she related how a relative who had been abusing her as her mother and husband had was taken totally by surprise when she bravely counterattacked. It was a breakthrough. She will still have to work hard because she has had a lifetime of behaving from her diminished self, but now she has her giant self to draw from.

The role of power and control is important in understanding unfinished business. It is your real or imagined lack of power which gives unfinished business its strength and staying power. As stated earlier, you were born with little real power to influence those around you and since humans have the longest dependency period of any animal, your real power was limited for many years.

Within these very real limits you were forced to make compromises with people, events, and institutions which often abused their powers over you. These powers became habitual patterns which you couldn't break because your basic survival depended upon meeting their demands.

At some point you had real power, but you didn't know how to use it. The rebelliousness of teenagers is a case in point. Of our seven children most of them went through this rebellion. The twins who were raised only by us, didn't. Why? From their earliest years we had total control over them. The others we shared with their other set of parents and we didn't have a chance to allow them to assume increasing power as they were ready.

Because we respected the twins, gave them gradually increasing responsibility even before they asked for it, gave them love and emotional support, they didn't have to rebel. If we abused them one of us recognized it and apologized and made it up to the child. Since they were allowed to challenge and confront us, always in a civil manner, they grew in strength and confidence and, with us, mostly operated at the level of their giant selves.

The earlier you can be helped to assert whatever your powers are at that moment in time, the less unfinished business will haunt you.

In almost all cases of unfinished business the person or persons had some real powers over you and abused them. A sense of injustice, frustration, anger or hatred lingers, but you are unable to express these feelings. Like a reverberating circuit the memories of the feelings circulate through your brain. Each time they do they reinforce the negative, diminished feelings. If, on top of what you are doing to yourself in your mind, these people actually continue to emotionally/mentally abuse you, it further strengthens your diminished self.

The worst part of unfinished business isn't just the negative pattern you have developed with the person who has diminished you, but the fact that you carry this pattern and attitude into other relationships. Therefore, if your father is overprotective you may be unable to generate initiative, but always wait until you're told what to do. If this fits the person with whom you're relating, then no overt problem arises. On the other hand, if your boss or boyfriend wants you to assert yourself and solve problems, you won't be able to function because you're trapped in unfinished business with your father.

My father died when I was nineteen. I was working through our power relationship. Before his death I had freed myself from my fears of him, but was trying to strongly establish an identity of my own which did not rely on his thoughts and feelings. His death left me no way to complete my gradual transition to accepting both his powers when it was appropriate and asserting my own when it was necessary as an expression of my giant self.

Consequently, I was frozen in a response to authority that was more negative than positive. In every job I held I challenged those who had legitimate authority over me. Each time I replayed the scenario in which I was attempting to free myself from my father. Because of my abilities and talents, I was respected, but I was disliked, because of the ways in which I challenged those in authority.

Ironically, I have benefited from this in that I became an astute observer and critic of power. It has enabled me to see beneath the facade and get to the heart of organizations and people. I would have been wealthier and would have gone through much less pain had my dad lived a few years longer. It is a trade-off which has had long-term benefits.

What can you do if, as in my case, the main person with whom you have unfinished business is dead?

Start with the imagery technique, relive the situations as you remember them, but with an awareness of errors due to your personal myth. Carefully think through the existing patters the deceased created in your behavior and how it has transferred to your behavior with the living.

Example: I was involuntarily transferred because of an allegedly personal feud with a principal. It was a complicated issue involving my twins, a few other teachers, and several local political issues, but it resulted in a transfer. The parents picketed the school for a month trying to get me back, but they were unsuccessful.

Actually, it was a good thing. I had fought for autonomy and had more freedom than any teacher I read about. Although I was very creative and gave the children an excellent program, I was so cocky that I tried whatever came to my mind. I seldom checked with any principal until after I'd worked out the bugs. If a program didn't work, I'd drop it before anyone knew about it. If it worked I had statistical or anecdotal proof so I could argue for its continuation.

The transfer proved that in the eyes of the district, I was just another teacher. Joe Liner, the principal of my new school, was (is) an exceptional person. He trusted people unless they proved themselves unworthy. He knew I'd been treated unjustly and said so. He respected my successes with children and told me that I could be as innovative as I wanted, but asked me to give him the respect he deserved by letting him know what I was doing and why.

With him it wasn't rhetoric. As long as you were effective he let you be yourself and teach in the ways you felt most comfortable. He was a man who operated from his giant self, not his diminished one. Therefore, I didn't fight with him nor did I hide things from him. Each time I got an idea I'd think it through so that I knew what I needed to do to apply it. I would briefly discuss it with him, answer any concerns he had, and, if his concerns were legal or logistic problems, I'd modify the idea.

It was a series of compromises between two adults who respected the expertise of one another. He kept everyone off my back and I rapidly improved my teaching which showed in the children's progress.

With the breakthrough with him I was able to more effectively deal with others in authority. There was a healthy change in my father-son authority pattern which had haunted me for years, especially with males or male-acting females.

Although in our first contact I had told him I was not impressed by the power of various authority figures, Joe had taken the initiative, taken command of the meeting. However, he also had shown respect for my needs and expertise. By doing this he and I had replaced the negative habit pattern I had with authority with a positive one in which we shared power.

Although I still showed obvious and overt disrespect to those in authority I felt were incompetent or inhuman, I gradually transferred my respect for him to others until I truly began to understand their behaviors.

To change any habitual pattern, you first have to recognize the pattern. Next, you must realize either who it started with and how it was transferred, or at least recognize its power over your life. You must understand that once you begin to consciously change any parts of the pattern, it can begin to unravel. As it does, you need to replace it with a more productive, healthy one. Then, like a road show, you need to try out the new pattern with as many different people as you can so that it becomes habitual.

This is not easy. I had unfinished business with my ex-father-in-law. I wrote him a long letter explaining my appreciation of the good things I felt he had done with one of my daughters while purposely not mentioning the damage I thought he had done to another. He never said anything about the letter, never wrote back, but from then on there was more friendship, concern, and comfort between us when we were together for occasions relating to my daughters.

My letter to him was also part of the healing of my unfinished business with my father, authority, and power. You can see that it works in both directions. When unfinished business isn't dealt with consciously, effectively, and cognitively to change the pattern, it continues to transfer to more and more people, building in power.

My relating to authority got increasingly worse and more complex as I rebelled against one authority figure after another. Unfinished business can snowball quickly or build over many years. It seldom gets better spontaneously because you impose the pattern on each succeeding person who seems to fit the pattern. As the number of people who become involved grows, the patterns also grows in greater depth and complexity making it easier for more people to fit into its limiting boundaries.

Part of the problem of unfinished business is that besides the insight and will necessary to change the pattern into another one, you are not willing to make the compromises, the trade-offs, to create a new behavior.

For most of my life I was unwilling to give up my angry, hostile behavior towards people who had legal or legitimate power over me. I took giving in to their authority as a sign of weakness on my part. I also felt that they were curtailing my creativity. The latter was true and had I given in I would not have discovered nor been able to pioneer much of what I've accomplished as a teacher. Now, I can accept others' opinions because they often make my task easier.

As a writer I refused to accept any criticism, which greatly limited my growth. Again, I was afraid my creativity would be compromised. In reality, it was a combination of problems with my personal myth and unfinished business with my father that prevented me from profiting from useful suggestions. This year I rewrote one book five times following what I recognized as helpful criticisms.

These changes did not come easily. Finding and accepting livable trade-offs takes thought, energy, courage, and will. It helps if you consider that these trade-offs are expressions of your giant self.

Seven

Trade-Offs: No Perfect Transactions

The thing that no one likes about compromises or trade-offs, is that everyone is certain to lose something that he wants. It doesn't matter that the other person is also losing something important. So there is no way that the trade-off can result in a perfect transaction. Each loses as well as gains. A trade-off is a conscious moving away from Black-White thinking.

The perfect transaction is one in which you get everything you want. Realistically, this turns out to be a you-win, he-loses proposition. Anytime the other person in a relationship feels he has lost, you have diminished him. A diminished person is not capable of love, loyalty, or any virtue or ability that could enhance you or your relationship.

It's true that an employer who pays his employee just enough to keep him working may feel that he is clever and a winner. However, his winning is at the expense of the employee. This employee will respond to the financial overtures of anyone who will pay him a few cents more.

The same is true of a marriage. If a man gives his wife just enough of himself to shut her up, she will be vulnerable to any sincere or predatory male who is willing to pay more attention to her.

The key to effective trade-offs is when both parties feel they have gained as much or more than they have lost. Each is intelligent, sensitive, and caring enough to work towards an equitable solution.

This is extremely difficult and is one reason relationships fall apart so easily and quickly. It is difficult because each one has his own agenda, beliefs, and perspective. Each feels he needs what he's asking for and tends to blame the other if the needs are not met.

Examples:

You marry a beautiful, talented, loving, and intelligent women who satisfies all your needs - except variety.

You stay single and have your phone book filled with fascinating women who meet all your needs - except feelings of stability, security, and uniqueness.

You buy the latest model car, but a year later there's a better one you cannot afford because of your large down payment.

You buy your wife candy, but she really wanted flowers.

You buy a pair of shoes because they're stylish, but they're not comfortable.

Every decision, whether conscious or unconscious, has trade-offs. The nature of any decision means evaluating, then eliminating or selecting some option in favor of others. But you often find that you didn't have all the facts and you regret your decision because it didn't get you what you wanted.

As you were defined and shaped by people and institutions on the basis of your diminished self, you were not trained to think in terms of trade-offs. You were taught that if you were really clever and carefully considered your decision, that you could make choices that would be perfect. You seldom think in terms of anything except what you want to happen. It leaves you vulnerable and unhappy when the clinkers appear.

Although a positive attitude towards an outcome can be healthy, it can be disastrous if it stops you from thinking about possible compromises, alternatives, and unpleasant side effects. You are unprepared and unable to cope with the inevitable unforeseen consequences of any decision.

Examples:

A woman marries a man who is financially secure. At first she is pleased because he showers her with gifts and she has more things than she ever dreamed of having. After awhile she finds that she needs increasingly interesting or expensive gifts until they too seem empty. He has been manipulating her diminished self. Her giant self needs her to be able to express her adult, not her child, her dependent self.

Entertainers, artists, athletes, all people who thirst for fame often find that the attention they yearned for has been paid for by the trade-off of lack of privacy. They thought they'd be freer, but became slaves of their fame.

Have you ever stood agonizing over which candy bar to buy? Do you select one, eat it, and then wish you had bought a different one?

I used to take Drixerol when I had a minor allergy attack at school. It's embarrassing and difficult to teach when your nose is dripping like a faucet. The medicine would stop the draining, but the trade-off was that it dried mucous membranes throughout my body. My colon would tear and bleed and urination would get increasingly difficult and painful. It was a trade-off I carefully considered.

School systems want the schools to be clean, quiet, and controlled because many people think these are important conditions for learning. The trade-off is that those who abide by these values often are constricted, fearful people who are unable to handle the complexities of modern life.

Some trade-offs Marie and I have made that have changed our lives are the following:

I think I was an excellent father. I listened to my children, gave them structure, support, and love, but tried to help them become increasingly independent. Although I had not thought of the giant self as a concept, I, and Marie worked towards that with the children. In the process I didn't read or work on my writing as much as I would have liked to do. It was a trade-off I adjusted to because I thought my day would come. It did. I began to enjoy some time to improve my craft as a writer.

Along came our grandchildren. I loved each one, but I had no intention of raising them as I had our children. Marie wanted to be more involved with them and expected me to feel and do the same. I was working a ten hour day with primary age children and the last person I wanted to see at five o'clock was another child with a high-pitched, whining voice. I resented the amount of time she spent with them because she wanted me to be with her and them, whereas I wanted her attention for myself.

We went through many angry and depressed moments as we negotiated and compromised until we came up with the trade-offs we could live with.

She could be with them as much as she wanted during the day, but the evenings were ours. I would spend quality time with them and give them more attention during the weekends. It was a general plan which each accepted but which could be changed occasionally if the events warranted it. It worked, but there were times when each of us felt he or she wasn't getting his or her fair share. But it was livable.

A larger issue concerned our roles in the marriage. We decided this before we got married. We agreed that she should stay at home and raise the children and I would bring in as much money as I could as a teacher. Since she wasn't contributing money to the household, she was to help me in frugally spending our limited resources.

Even though I always had extra jobs, we never made it through a year without borrowing money. She and I seldom spent a cent on ourselves or each other. We agreed that the children came first. Most of the time this worked, but there were times we wanted something for the other or ourselves which made our agreement very difficult to live with. It was during these times that we felt the trade-off was choking us.

A frequent problem in relationships is commitment of time to one another. In the beginning most couples want to spend each moment together. As they become more secure, one or both may want more time alone, at work, at play, or just with others. The one who feels he needs more space often poses a threat to the other. The one most threatened and insecure negotiates for the most time. The other must discover a trade-off in which he has the most freedom without destroying the relationship. The more insecure one must compromise, but not give in. The negotiation and discussion must continue until each has lost something of value, but gained enough to keep the relationship alive and growing.

Without the give and take of trade-offs most relationships either end or one member gets his needs met while the other is dominated. Domination may be through the alleged helplessness of the supposedly weaker one having his honor and/or guilt played upon. In the relationship each should be able to retain his personal power and continue to grow as a person.

However, each has to realize that besides his own identity he is part of a couple. He has a responsibility to the couple as well as to his own identity and the trade-off process is one way this goal is accomplished. It is through the conscious, thoughtful negotiations necessary for any livable trade-offs that relationships truly flower into mature, long-lasting love.

One of the things that prevent livable trade-offs -- and I must emphasize the importance of livable -- is that egoholism interferes with negotiations and compromises.

Eight

Egoholism: Me First, Me Only

An egoholic is a person who constantly thinks and acts as if he were the only one in the world with needs to be met. His behavior says "me first and me only." Like an alcoholic, foodaholic, or drug addict he is gripped in an obsession. He is preoccupied with satisfying himself.

Marie and I were overwhelmed with the intensity of the obsessions our overweight clients had with food. Every one of them cheated or seriously deviated from his individual diet plan contract. When I treated alcoholics in the Air Force, I had to search their gear and area daily, but they managed to get and stash bottles in clever and unbelievable places.

All these people somehow tied or associated their obsessional needs with a specific mode of relief. Without their daily fix or fixes they became anxious and fearful. Their diminished selves were the main determiners of their actions -- not logic, thoughtfulness, or anything emanating from their sleeping giant selves. An egoholic is the same. He needs to have his ego fixes because he is so fearful of losing any part of his shaky identity that he is unable to allow himself to see or meet any one else's needs.

It is like watching a very young child. Because of his helplessness a child is similar to a baby bird. His needs are made obvious by his open mouth which is continuously open begging for others to meet his needs. A child has difficulty comprehending any one else's needs because his are so overwhelming to him. He has little sympathy for the thoughts or feelings of others until his needs are met. This is the behavior of an egoholic.

In an adult or adolescent, egoholism is regressive behavior or stunted growth. He has not moved from the helplessness of a child to the mature interdependence of an adult. I said interdependence, because no social being is ever totally independent nor should he be totally dependent. He interacts with others making livable trade-offs within reasonable expectations. He needs others and takes what he deserves as well as gives them what they want and earn. The egoholic takes as much as he can and gives as little as he can in return.

Every day I tell Marie that I love her. It is a statement that is earned and deserved. I praise her cooking, the garden or house, her looks, or in some ways show my appreciation for all the things she does for me, our children, and others. My behavior is not egoholic nor manipulative as is most egoholism, but is a way to maturely express my love. My statements come from my giant self. If I made them just to get her to do something for me without regard for her feelings then it would be from my diminished self.

Egoholics are self-centered and self-preoccupied but they are not self-confident. Only a person with a diminished self thinks only of himself. One who operates from his giant self meets his needs while meeting the needs of others too.

When I write a beautiful poem, teach an exciting lesson, or help another person see himself more clearly, I have earned and expect my strokes. Some of the strokes I give to myself because my giant self can honestly appraise my behavior and can give me what I have earned. I can also accept deserved praise from others.

Because I am self-confident and competent I compliment others when I see them look well or do something I believe is deserving of praise. It gives me great satisfaction to know how much pleasure my comments and compliments bring to others. It's nice when I get some in return, but I know my growth is more dependent upon what I give than what I receive. The giving should and does give me immense joy. It is its own reward in that my giant self is fed by these actions. However, I am not so secure that I can continue to give without receiving. If after I have given to a person, but he has not given me anything in return, I will not turn the other cheek, but will treat him as he deserves.

Such a person is probably an egoholic because he is incapable of giving praise or anything else unless he sees a direct benefit from his actions. An egoholic is such a fearful, miserable person that he cannot squeeze compassion or thoughtfulness towards others out of his tiny ego. He feels constantly diminished and so covers up by bluster, smoke screens, and a total inability to listen to or see others and their needs. He is endlessly searching for emotional support and tries to get his ego stroked by anyone or anything. He lives for these fixes. But like any fix, it has to be frequent and the dosage raised periodically as his dependency grows.

I'm certain that from my definition you see that at least part of your behavior could be classed as egoholic. You need others. You need their praise, support, and love. How do you differentiate between egoholism and the normal expression of a healthy ego with its normal needs?

An egoholic is a non-listener. He is a manipulator of others in that he gives them as little as possible of himself but is an expert in getting the most from them. He is seldom willing to put himself out for others. Often he feels persecuted and thinks the world owes him a living because he may have suffered as a child. He is neither independent nor interdependent but is dependent. In his dependency he wants and expects others to meet his insatiable needs. This insatiability, this "me first, me only" obsession with his needs, is a sign of egoholism.

I know that you also want praise, affection and love on a constant basis. I do too. However, I am willing to listen to others, to try and meet their needs as they see them, to care about their feelings, and to earn their praise and love. Then, if they do not respond, I have some realistic basis for my disappointments.

Therefore, I have choices. I can assert and express my giant self because that is me. Those who respond in kind engage me in a healthy exchange of support and love. Those who cannot I can either try to help or I can let them stew in their own self-made misery soup. Often I will confront them with how I see our shared reality. With some it shocks them into change, with others there is only anger. Life is a risk and I'm willing to take it.

Example: When I go to a new school I am friendly with everyone. I assume the best of everyone and meet each student and adult with a smile and greeting. Many people are confused by my openness and, at first, many do not return my smile or greeting. I assume that this is because I intimidate them and they need time to get used to me. After awhile, I know those prune-faces with the tiny egos cannot give sunshine because they have dried up inside. I may stop greeting them or, my diminished self may encourage me to make a point of my greetings because I know it makes them uncomfortable. No one's perfect and revenge does have a sweet quality to the diminished me.

An egoholic doesn't risk. The people who spurned my enthusiasm demonstrated their fears. They were afraid that if they gave to me, either I would disappoint them, or they thought if I got to know them I would be disappointed and not continue our friendship. There are those who treat me as an inferior because they have more money, more power, are part of the social whirl, or find my ethnicity or beliefs beneath them. These are people with constipation of the brain.

Relationships are risky. It takes a strong ego to make the trade-offs and not have unrealistic expectations. An egoholic does not have a strong ego, just strong demands. He is a scavenger setting up people so he can feast on their labors and skills without risking or giving of himself.

Egoholism is part of a continuum that goes from egoholism, to self-confidence, to self-awareness, to self-realization and spiritual transcendence. A person moves gradually away from total dependence and fear to independence and self-confidence to interdependence, responsibility, and creative self-expression, and self-actualization.

Yet successful self-actualized people still may have a sense of emptiness. It may be what pushes them towards creative endeavors. They learn to enjoy the process of creativity, growth, and problem-solving, but find it is addicting, insatiable. This is one of the reasons that these creative people try to lose themselves in other addictions or lose themselves in other people, often through sex.

What is missing is spiritual transcendence. This is the wish to merge with the Ineffable, the Unknowable, the No Thing Ness That Is All, Allah, God, or whatever you call Him or It that is beyond your imagination to conceptualize.

The polar opposite of egoholism is any kind of spirituality which allows you to forgo your ego and its needs and blend into the Infinite. Spiritual transcendence goes beyond the human, social, and ecological altruism of self-awareness and self-actualization in which you have created yourself and generously give of yourself in the constant healthy exchanges of interdependency.

Spiritual transcendence is the discipline of going beyond the fears and pettiness of your ego and the ego needs of others. It is the letting go of all ego. Meditation seems to be the way many who have achieved this level have traveled. This is the ultimate expression of your spiritual development and should take you beyond your obsessional and insatiable ego needs which typify most humans.

I make no pretence of having reached this level. If I had, I wouldn't be writing this book which reflects a lower level of human evolution. I can, like you, simultaneously work on more than one level while I use my giant self to progress towards higher levels. However, there can be no progress towards self-confidence, self-awareness, self-actualization, and spiritual transcendence until you break the strangling bonds of egoholism. Possibly, if you understood just how truly unique you are, it would be easier to free yourself. Read on to see how incredibly unique you are.

Nine

Your Uniqueness!
Universally: One-Of-A-Kind

At conception the mix of your parents genes created a unique combination which had never before occurred nor would ever occur again in exactly the same way. In all the Universe there was, is, and will be no one exactly like you.

The infinite combinations the genes can take have certain predetermined possibilities. Those involved in shaping the nose usually are similar to one or both parents' noses. They could shape one somewhat like a distant relative or like no one else in your ancestry. The chances of a child born in a Scandinavian country of having a nose with wide nostrils would be rare because most of the genes from his gene pool come from thin-nostriled people. Yet, it could happen. The chance of his nose being wrinkled and shaped like an elephant's trunk would be zero because these characteristics are not part of the human gene pool.

Some scientists believe that from conception to birth every child mimics evolution in that each begins from a simple single-celled animal and progresses through most major phyla or classifications until he arrives at the highest point as a human. Because of this, when something goes wrong with the original random gene combinations or anything that occurs in utero to upset the delicate chemical instructions, a child could develop the appearance of a subhuman. Some children are born with features or traits that seem more animal than human.

These mutations creating animal-appearing humans or human-appearing animals pose an interesting question. Are they human or animal? If the level of consciousness and ability to make choices are the main dividing lines between humans and lower animals, some of these physically and mentally deformed persons would not fit into a human classification. This may not endear me to some readers, but science has gradually eroded all the differences between humans and other animals except the quality of our consciousness and our ability to make choices based on something other than instinct, genetics, and social conditioning. This means that all the differences between humans and other animals are quite blurred except in the quality of our thinking. If this becomes the standard then many people now labeled human would no longer be considered so. It could be used as a way to justify various abortions, voluntary euthanasia, and merciful deaths of those who were human, but are now brain-dead or no longer "human."

One thing I am attempting in this book is to free your thinking. In this way you can reprogram or reimprint yourself the way you want to be. This means being able to think the unthinkable. This does not mean you must think like me, nor do you need to act upon your thoughts. If you cannot think new thoughts you will be frozen in time and space and will have your body in the 21st Century, but your mind and actions in the 19th Century.

So you are born looking more like your parents and ancestors because their genes have placed certain reasonable limits upon what you can be. Two African pygmies are not going to give birth to a child who could grow into a seven-foot, red-haired Caucasian. Most children are born with all the appropriate body parts and internal organs.

However, because people all have hearts, livers, brains, and the necessary structures which differentiate them from other species does not mean there is not an almost impossible-to-imagine difference between individual people.

As a parent of seven and a teacher who has worked with thousands I am constantly amazed at the differences in understanding and responses to exactly the same set of directions. Of course motivation and interest as well as other extrinsic factors play a part, but the internal chemistry (the genetic givens) of each are underplayed because they are too complicated.

When we look at a group of ten year-old children and ask them to run a hundred yard dash we know there will be a range in time from thirteen to twenty plus seconds. We know this because we can see the physical differences in size, body shape, coordination, and general physical strength. We cannot see their insides, their internal chemistry in which the differences are much greater.

If we hold up an apple and ask the color, the children respond with, "red." However, each sees the red somewhat differently. When light hits the retina, rhodopsin is split into two parts, opsin and retinene. When a person is deficient in vitamin A, less retinene is available for the formation of visual purple. The cones also contain another pigment, visual violet, which is also dependent on vitamin A. Each student has ingested varying amounts of vitamin A which could make a difference in the redness he sees. Even if students all took in the exact same amount of vitamin A their bodies could process and effectively utilize it differently based on the complex biochemical interactions that occur even in the simplest physiological processes. Therefore, in a class of thirty children staring at a red apple the concept of "redness" may be shared, but what is actually being seen and experienced by each child may be vastly different.

What happens when an almost microscopic amount of LSD is ingested? It sends a flurry of biochemical reactions throughout the body, totally changing "reality." If a small amount of a chemical can change your body what do you think your daily food intake does to it? Each bite is biochemical dynamite which explodes through millions of cells, tissues, organs, and systems causing constant changes.

Beginning with your unique combination of genes, further compounded by your unique life in utero, accelerated by the various external environments and experiences, you become more unique. You get even more and more unique doing the most ordinary human activities such as eating, sleeping, and communicating with other humans.

Based strictly on the genetic givens, in utero experiences, and then your reactions (choices) to your environments, there is no one like you. As you gain life experiences these differences become more pronounced because it isn't just the physiological differences that come into play, but the sociological, psychological, and spiritual which make you more unique.

Two reasons for this chapter: One is to make you aware of your uniqueness by virtue of your existence alone. Obviously, the more you take charge of your life and its directions, the greater your uniqueness. If you believe and understand this, it may make you less frantic in your quest to be unique. Without effort you are unique already. With effort, you only widen the gaps between you and others.

Secondly, if you grasp your physiological and then your psychological and sociological uniqueness, you may understand better why it is so difficult for you to communicate to other humans. It's true you have many commonalties and it's through these that you are able to understand and be understood. However, if you can fathom your complexity, you should be more tolerant of the human complexity of those with whom you are trying to communicate.

You are an incredibly complex unique human. Remember that everyone you meet is also incredibly complex and unique. I believe if you begin from that viewpoint, you will, from this moment on, drastically change your life.

Why? How? When you believe this, then the constant put-downs that occur in your daily life are less potent. After all, the nature of a put-down is its ability to make you feel less human, less unique. By following and believing my argument proving your uniqueness, no one can permanently make you feel less human. (I'm aware that people will still insult or degrade you, belittle you in words or deeds, but all you need to do is realize they're playing to your diminished self and you need to draw upon your giant self). This can be done by remembering how incredibly unique you are. Your sense of yourself should enable you to more fully develop all the potentials of your giant self. Feeling unique you do not need to constantly clamor for bits and pieces of attention from others to validate yourself. You can do it for yourself and thereby accelerate your growth in many areas.

Validating yourself could change your life because you won't need to put others down to build yourself up. Feeling unique and good about yourself, you should be extremely generous with yourself and giving to others. Giving should spill from you like a bottle filled to overflowing.

When I began to really feel this way, I tried it out by complimenting strangers. I'd done it for years with friends and co-workers, but the acid test for me, because I'm basically shy, was with strangers. My virgin attempt was a disaster. I saw a very distinguished man exiting a store. He had a perfectly groomed mustache, beard, and flowing white hair. I stopped him to comment, but I got flustered, blurted out an incomprehensible phrase, and he looked at me as if I were either gay or a complete ass. I have gotten much better and can compliment anyone without appearing as if I'm trying to hit on or insult him/her.

Sincerely believing and understanding your uniqueness frees you to be in frequent contact with your giant self. In this frame of mind you will find that you will be able to contact the giant self that is in all the others you meet.

It is not easy. Much of the rest of the book deals with other ways to see yourself and others so that you can operate more and more in the mind set of your giant self.

In order to communicate this mind set more effectively, let's examine language next.

Ten

Language! Frozen Patterns

Like mathematics, every language has its own very specific patterns. Each has its own rhythms, intonations, and has a surface and a deep structure. The surface structure is the obvious meaning from the literal shared meanings attributed to the sound patterns. The deep structure has all the emotional shadings and nuances of meaning that a person unfamiliar with the language would miss or not appreciate. This deep structure involves more than the idioms which are language usages which those unfamiliar with the language miss. It is composed of many things like the slight emphasis of a syllable or tone which takes the words far afield from their literal meanings. A man could be seductive, insulting, or complimentary using the exact same words but with subtle voice or bodily nuances. Language structure is also reflective of the speaker's and listener's intelligence and intuition.

The surface structure of a language can be taught through grammatical, syntactical, pronunciation, and syllabication rules. (Not all languages can be lumped into these generalizations.) However, no one learns his primary language in this way. It is now believed that babies are born with an inherited, evolutionary ability to learn language. This ability is built into the structure of their brains and nervous systems.

Once the child is exposed to his language's specific patterns he becomes imprinted or programmed by them. As if he were using a sieve or template he allows only those patterns to enter into his awareness which fit his understanding and expectations of sounds and meanings. He becomes increasingly shaped by his primary language. If he has had a dog or dogs and has many happy, sad, and other emotional reactions because of his real experiences with dogs, the word "dog" may cause any one of several physical feelings to occur within him. Even if he learns *perro* and *hundt* from other languages these words which mean dog will not create the exact same feelings because his language has frozen these patterns into his neurological, bodily structure.

Read S. I. Hayakawa, Stuart Chase, or Alfred Korzybski and you will learn that each language, by its nature and structure, creates in its users very specific views of reality. It allows the users to share a commonality, a bonding which would not be possible if each sound meant something different. However, the trade-off is that each language freezes the users' flexibility. It is very difficult for them to see other, equally valuable realities, which can only be seen if the bonds of the deep language structure are loosened.

I was raised the first few years of my life as an Orthodox Jew. The word "gentile" in the dictionary means a non-Jew. That is its surface structure. The way it was used in my family in St. Paul during the Thirties (the Depression...the time of Hitler's rise to power...) the deep structure meant "enemy, danger, fear." It took me almost forty years to dilute its emotional loading so that I can respond to it on the basis of its surface structure.

It was one of the words that negatively shaped my reactions to authority -- usually a Gentile who, in my mind, was abusing me. My family, using this word and many more like it, imprinted, froze in my brain structures, the belief that these people were not to be trusted and would hurt me.

Watch how powerfully words have imprinted you. Remember all these words are just written signs for specific sounds which have taken symbolic-emotional meaning to you.

Nigger! You are a nigger. You smell like a nigger. You are a beaner. You are lazy and worthless. Commie, you are a traitor to your country. Kike, you smell like all your rotting relatives in the camps. Queer, you love to suck dirty cocks. Pig, you're so fat you must eat everything in sight, even shit.

I apologize, but I think I made my point. Words are not mere sounds puffed into the air, but create very, very specific realities. Even though you probably clearly understood why I used them, my use of these words may have turned you against me. If they did, if you cannot respect or like me because of what I just wrote, then, well, you are a pathetic, brained-washed, idiot.

Ha! Gotcha again! Seriously, it is impossible not to react emotionally to some words. To be human is to be frozen in these language patterns.

Forty years ago my father and I were involved in Dianetics. We bought a machine which was a psycho-galvanometer, but we didn't know it. Its purpose was to help us find the engrams locked in people's brains. We had gone through the training to do so. We were Clears. This meant that we could help others deprogram themselves. The machine measured the amount of sweat on a client's palms like a lie-detector does.

Recent discoveries in neuroanatomy have made the ideas of engrams almost a fact. When a word is received by your brain it changes the sound energy into electrochemical energy responses which travel through your nervous system. The brain cells create a physiological, biochemical pattern which then functions like Hubbard's conception of an engram. The engram was a pattern frozen in the physical structure of your brain.

Hubbard believed that the intensity of galvanic response meant that the Clear had found the word or phrase that was the semantic equivalent of the physical engram. By having the client repeat the phrase over and over, its emotional charge would quickly be defused and he would be cured. He was betting that it would be extinguished, but sometimes repetition reinforced it and the client was more firmly entrenched with it. Dianetics was a simplistic answer to a complex problem which is why it failed more than it succeeded.

The pleasant or positive memories and meanings of words are equally important shapers of your reality. Certain words associated with my wife, my children, sex, sports, or foods always bring me pleasure and happiness. Combinations like Marie, sex, and food are most heavily happy.

Your ego or self is shaped by your language. Certain Indian tribes have a language structure that doesn't allow them to express the idea that they are the cause or creators of their actions. The action happens to them and they are merely the vehicles through which the action occurs. It is a nice way to avoid what we call responsibility for their actions. Yet, they do not have the sense of a self that is separated from others as we do. They are part of their tribe or village just as a bee is part of the hive. Their lives serve the greater good of the community. It is through the community that they draw a sense of themselves.

Our egos are tied up in meeting our own needs first and foremost. Because of this our sense of our own mortality is frightening. Since these Indians' selves are bound with the community, their death will not mean the end of that which is most important -- the community. Our death means extinction, unless we have a faith that takes us beyond our temporary existence. However, since responsibility is important if we are to be the designers of our fate and of the evolution of our species, to us the sense of self and of control is more important than being just a cog in the wheel of the community. Either concept can be seen as right or wrong, but that is not the issue. The issue is that language controls how you see and define your reality.

All these ideas emanate from our uses of language. In each case the language is shading the ideas as well as the ideas shading the language. It isn't just in abstract or philosophical issues or words that this happens but even in concrete or factual ones.

Take the word snow. We use it mainly as a noun describing it as an entity, an object. At times we see it both as a name for something tangible, a noun, and as a gerund, as when it is snowing. We physically see the snow in very specific and limiting ways. An Eskimo sees it in a much more varied and profound way. He has over one hundred fifty words and phrases with which his language deals with snow. His environment shaped his language, but his language also shaped how he sees his environment. Because of the nature of his language he actually, physically can more easily see the snow much differently than we can which enables him to live with it more effectively.

Of course, a word's meanings are always in some context and so the setting in which it is embedded makes a difference. Denotation and connotation need to be considered.

The denotation of a word is the exact, literal meaning, whereas connotation suggests or implies added meanings. The denotation of slender or skinny is thin, but slender connotes approval and skinny, disapproval. White denotes a color which contains all the visible rays of the spectrum, but it may connote such qualities as purity and holiness. Black denotes absence of color, but its connotative meaning in most white cultures is bad or evil. Therefore, the connotative meaning of black is a language usage that freezes prejudice in the thinking and speech of non-blacks. Unfortunately, it did the same to the black minority which is why they have elected to call themselves Blacks and hopefully eradicate the negative uses of the word.

One more example of how language freezes thought and limits actions: If your parents and relatives labeled you "stupid" by tying this word to many different experiences and behaviors, the following probably has happened. Your reality was shaped by the word. It has an attitude associated with it and it may have developed into a self-fulfilling prophecy for you and them. Every time you made a human error, you were labeled. After awhile, every mistake you made even when no one else was around resulted in your labeling yourself stupid, thereby constantly reinforcing the word and subsequent actions.

You cannot escape your language and its imprints, but you can recognize them so you can modify their impact. Your very awareness of how it works permanently softens the strong metaphor of this chapter. By realizing that your language is just one window into realities and that you can change your realities by changing how you use language, you can permanently defrost your childhood imprints and conditioning.

In my classes I work harder than most teachers against capping, ragging, and teasing that tends to reinforce all the negative language experiences of the children. I am trying to do the same for you. If you will become aware of every time you belittle others or examine your religion, politics, or philosophy so that they do not continue to be belittling to others, you will discover a freedom and happiness you never believed existed.

If at the same time you begin to learn a new language with the idea of further freeing yourself, you will begin to see more and more how your language has frozen your thinking into limiting patterns of thought and behavior.

If you can admit now how your language limits you and leads you into error, read on and see how your brain, out of necessity, does even worse. This too can be remedied -- to a degree.

Eleven

Your Brain Leads You Into Constant Error

What a depressing chapter heading! The bright side is once you understand how and why the brain leads you into error you will be able:

1) to recognize the error as it's happening or soon after;
2) to thoughtfully search for more information;
3) to rethink your position;
4) to better reconstruct your feelings; and
5) to evaluate people and situations more clearly so your decisions and actions are more congruent with the larger picture.

First of all, if you think your brain is some sort of objective, dispassionate observer of events which calmly takes in information and then makes logic, rational decisions, you're in LaLaLand. We all like to think we make decisions like that, but our brains don't work that way.

That magnificent monument to millions of years of evolution, that wonder of the ages, is the biggest error-making organ ever created. Think of it from a statistical viewpoint. The more information anything carries, the more decisions an entity must make, human, animal, or machine, the more errors are statistically possible. Every moment of your life your brain is taking in millions of information bits and it must immediately decide how much attention it must pay to each, organize it in some category to make some sense of it, and decide what to do with it. It must make many decisions immediately and simultaneously, such as: how much of the rest of the brain and body should be involved?; should this information be stored in short or long-term memory?; where should it be stored; what other parts of the body/mind need to be alerted?; how does it fit with previous experiences?

Think of one of the brain's functions as that of a receptionist. A good receptionist is a competent filter. She answers all incoming calls and decides whether or not her organization should deal with them. If she thinks it's appropriate she will then decide who should handle this information. She may also decide to save, store, and then give the information to the correct person if he is out or busy at that time. If it's a wrong number or inappropriate information, she will discard it. However, if it later becomes appropriate, she may well add the previous information to a current message to increase its usefulness.

She may transfer the call or person to the secretary who is a higher level filter. She is also a pattern detector or classifier like the receptionist. Each has to decide both to say yes or no to the call (filter) and then decide where or to whom it goes (classification or pattern detection.) Each secretary serves one or more middle managers. She protects them from unnecessary information that would waste their precious time and energy. When she does pass it on to one of them, she feels he is the best person to handle it.

The middle manager has the power to act upon the data. He interprets its usefulness to the organization and releases more information (as the body releases hormones and enzymes) which directs his subordinates to carry out his instructions. Their actions then contribute to the success of the organization (as organs and muscles do something to benefit the body).

This is again very simplistic. In essence there are many receptionists and secretaries operating simultaneously in the brain because the incoming information comes from every sense organ, including the skin and muscles, as well as the constant internal messages coming from every cell, tissue, organ, and system in the body. That is why a comparison between a computer and a human have some metaphorical usefulness, but the metaphor doesn't match reality.

It's as if all these millions of messages are handled by thousands of receptionists and secretaries each second. They filter and classify the messages and send them on to the middle managers who handle the majority of them. Higher order or more complicated decisions are not handled by one chief executive, but by a committee of them. Each is in control of part of the responses.

Suppose you wish to get out of your chair. Your eyes may survey the area to see if there is room to move. Your ears may listen to determine if anyone is around you. Your muscular-skeletal systems determine the physics of getting up. Your cerebellum and inner ear must compensate so you won't fall forward. Your hypothalamus and pituitary glands combine to send the appropriate messages to your blood stream to stimulate the release of sugars which may come from protein or carbohydrate storages. The situation will determine how much of what enzymes and minerals will be necessary for each specific reaction. Your heart will need to be told to beat faster.

And, this high level committee is like a gigantic emergency war room in which all the incoming data after being filtered, classified, and reacted upon needs to be constantly evaluated. This means that each member of the executive committee has to carefully listen to the reactions of each of the other committee members' decisions and then, in a constant feedback loop, immediately determine his next move.

Getting up from your chair is exponentially more complicated than I've described. Can you imagine any such operation being error-free? You've been in organizations. Do any of them run without error? I rest my case.

I'll simplify the matter. Suppose the brain did allow data in one bit at a time like the neat digital computer model we all like to use. The receptionist, secretary, middle (is it muddle?) manager, and executive each would have to make sense of it as soon as he/she received it. Remember, each bit is still coming at them with blinding speed and a decision has to be made immediately. (When has an organization you've seen ever worked that quickly?)

Therefore, each classifies or groups the bit into some category or place which is familiar to her/him. No matter how chaotic the bit appears the filter or pattern detector will force a place for it. Of course, the bit may be rejected as noise or non-information, but if at all possible it will be processed.

The process of fitting a bit of information into a category, we call classifying. This means selecting from its attributes or characteristics, assigning more importance to some than others, and then deciding to what category the bit belongs. This is largely dependent on our past experiences. We fit these bits into familiar classes. Errors can occur in the perception of various attributes, in determining the impact of each, and in organizing them into the correct category.

The process of missing, ignoring, or inappropriately categorizing and then forcing the data to fit into arbitrary categories is called rationalization. This enables us to constantly use any bit of information to fit any belief we previously held. Every human being does this, no matter how intellectually gifted, how emotionally controlled, or how spiritual he is. This tendency is built into the normal workings of his brain. Why?

Think in terms of our total evolution, not as a person in the Information Age. Up until a few thousand years ago, the majority of our dangers were immediate. Since we were not as dependent on instincts as other animals, we had to have a brain that made complex decisions almost instantly. These were usually based on limited information. The potentially deep thinkers of those times, those who carefully evaluated data, ended up as topsoil. Evolution doesn't easily give up something which is effective. A brain that processes an enormous amount of information can respond to more varied and complex situations than one which is dependent on instinct for minimal programs. Therefore, as language and social organizations became more effective as means for individual survival, the older evolutionary responses were no longer useful. Unfortunately, they were still part of the brain wiring and patterns from the past.

So, the brain in our information age must process a prodigiously greater amount of information, though not with life-or-death situations as its predecessors of several thousand years had to do. It's like forcing a soldier to become a philosopher. Most humans react without taking into consideration all the complications and consequences. I'm saying this because of the evolutionary nature of the brain.

It's similar to the way the so-called reptilian or primitive brain operates. It is composed of the brain stem and nervous system and, as is true with all organs or systems, it cooperates with other parts of the brain and body to do its job. Its job is to control respiration, heart beat, and many of involuntary systems of the body. These can also be controlled by the cortical brain, but it is more efficient to allow the reptilian brain to function without the interference of the higher brain. However, in certain cases dealing with stress and diseases, it has been discovered that through meditation and visualization the higher brain can change or modify the functioning of the primitive brain to improve the health of the person.

This can also be true with the way the higher order cortical brain processes incoming data. By realizing its once useful speed is no longer necessary in a society where complex factors need to be weighed before decisions are made, you can, through conscious control and will, monitor and modify your brain's initial reactions. By recognizing that your tendency is to make rapid decisions based on inadequate data and then to force them, to rationalize them, to fit your preconceived notions, you can permanently alter your behaviors.

Example: Nigger. The word is emotionally loaded and means many different things depending on the color of your own skin, certain other physical features, whether the label has been applied to you, your socioeconomic status, your actual contacts with people so labeled, your education, your contacts with opinions about "niggers" which you were imprinted by TV, the media, and the general fears and misconceptions about Blacks that have been "in the air" for four centuries.

The male members of my family transferred that prejudice to me, but my mother and other female members raised me to evaluate people by their relations with me. I was educated by teachers in Minnesota and Wisconsin who were less prejudiced than the materials they were forced to use.

Therefore, I had a confusing melange of messages. Because my first contacts with Blacks were all positive, I tended to react with the imprints from the females in my family. This enabled me (my cortical brain) to be more patient and tolerant of behaviors which would have "proven" the accuracy of the beliefs of the males in my family. It enabled me to evaluate each Black I met on the basis of his humanity and individuality rather than burden him with the prejudices inherent in the generalization "nigger."

The first day a child is fidgety in school, the teacher's initial reaction is "hyperactivity." This label seems to be based on solid information, but it is a limited cortical brain and mostly an emotional brain reaction on the part of the teacher. It is easy for the teacher to generalize and then rationalize that he is acting "for the good of the child." Everyone supports the teacher's error and the child is labeled and his life limited by a human error created by an outmoded evolutionary reaction supported by modern "research" (substitute rationalization).

The practice of counting to ten before you speak when you think you're going to say or do something you regret can be applied here. There is no way you will ever have "all" the information necessary in making a correct generalization. If you know that your brain forces you to make generalizations based on limited data which lead you into constant error, then you can make them just as you always have. The difference is that after you do, you do not act until you've examined your mind and heart. After you have thought through your options and made your best choice, still be aware that errors are possible. Keep your mind open and listen for feedback so you may further modify your choices.

If you're a king, leader, or master of your castle, ignore this entire section. People expect you to respond quickly and be constantly wrong and rigid. Then you can be blamed for everything that goes wrong. It's a pattern built into their brains, and yours too. Whether ye be a king or commoner, be ye aware that ye are not only lied to by yer evolutionary brain, but by every one of yer senses!

Twelve

Your Senses: Multiple Illusions

Into your wonderfully unique, extraordinary body/brain comes a constant onslaught of sensations like heat, cold, pressure of objects, and feel of things against your skin. The sounds of birds, trains, language of love, the wind, every pleasant or irritating sound enters your ears. You see the shapes of words, colors of foods, the unbelievable beauty of your lover. You taste the saltiness of her sweat, the sweetness of ice cream, the sourness of a pickle, and the bitterness of aspirin. Yet, is what you feel, taste, smell, hear, and see exactly the same as what you think you are perceiving from "out there," beyond the limits of your body?

Dorothy Lee, a cultural anthropologist, after studying how many cultures see the same reality differently does believe there is a single reality "out there." I agree and I assume you do too or you wouldn't be reading this book. If this reality has "seeable" dimensions then they should be "seen" by every human exactly the same. Wrong! This would be a reasonable possibility if every person was exactly alike and had exactly the same experiences. No two humans can see exactly the same reality since, if you agree with the chapter on your uniqueness, no two humans have the same genetic givens nor do they interact with their environments in the same way.

Given the fact that each person is physiologically, biochemically different it is another reasonable assumption that each person will "see," perceive, or receive through his senses everything in the external environment with a slight to an enormous degree of difference from everyone else. Given this fact is it any wonder that humans argue passionately, angrily, and futilely about the differences in what they see. Each "knows" what he sees (and he is correct, to some degree) and assumes that what the other person says he "sees" means that;

1) the other person is a liar, a fool, or just wrong, or
2) the other person assumes he is a liar, a fool, or just wrong.

Neither one or two are acceptable to most of us.

However, my point is more than we each see every object differently, but that we are often deceived by our senses and so, in truth, we seldom see exactly what is "out there." I've said that our language, whatever it is, actually freezes in space/time much of what we see. But it's even worse, our sense receptors, our organs of perception are unable to give us an exact picture of what is "out there."

As a child you were tricked with visual illusions. Two lines were shown in different contexts and you "saw" them as larger, the same, or smaller than they were. Magicians depend upon the inability of the eye to see what you think it's seeing to trick you. Escher, the artist, is a master at tricking our eyes into seeing different things in the same picture.

In a cavernous room full of people listening to an operatic soprano who has a range of five octaves, each will hear her differently. It would depend upon how far he is away from her, his musical sophistication and knowledge of the arias, the health of the hair follicles in his ears' cochlea which could affect what he is capable of hearing and transmitting to his brain, and his motivation/attention during her performance.

While eating a spicy dish using hot peppers, there is a range of one to two hundred thousand times the necessary amount of capsaicin necessary to taste the hotness dependent upon how many nerve cells have been destroyed in previous experiences with green peppers. An experienced hot pepper eater would swear (correctly for him) that a dish was mild while a virginal eater could be experiencing real pain as the capsaicin was killing nerve endings.

As a chocoholic I can detect differences in flavor and texture of chocolates that others don't. Scotch drinkers can tell brands and will look at you with disgust if you try to pawn off one that doesn't fit their acquired tastes.

All this is why you should be careful when suggesting foods or restaurants to others. What tastes exquisite to you may cause puzzlement, irritation, or illness to others.

Such differences can be a major problem in families. Suppose you're a young Jewish girl of forty years ago raised with all the chicken fat and butters used in cooking then. If you were low in the manufacture of bile (which breaks fat into small globules) or the lipases (enzymes that break fat down) you would have been so gassy they would have to have fed you outside with the dog. No one would have thought that you had a different metabolism of fatty foods, but would have made you feel guilty or an outcast.

Children have mild to major allergies to foods they both like and dislike. Parents become angry when children don't eat what they're given and accuse them of willfulness (which is still a possibility) when it may be differences in biochemistry.

Besides the physiological differences which cause you to see the same objects or events differently, there is the added burden placed upon you by your culture. That is, what you're taught to see or believe will affect what you see.

When I taught at an almost all Black school, I was one of the white people who treated the children like persons of worth. They liked me as much as I liked them. Since most of their contacts with whites had been negative, it was difficult for them to believe that I could be white and a good, likeable person. Therefore, many of the children refused to believe I was white and told me and others that I was a Mexican. They could not force their minds to see me as black, but they knew enough light-skinned, dark-haired Mexicans to place me in that category.

An experiment done several decades ago asked a group of whites to explain what was happening on a train. A young black was apparently angry at a white person on a train. Although he had no weapon a large number of people "saw" a razor in his hand. This and other experiments and observations after that confirmed the fact that prejudice and other culturally induced misconceptions can lead to exactly the same kinds of errors of perceptions as do differences in the biochemistry of the senses.

This is an excellent example of how your cultural mindset allows you to reorganize the incoming sensory impulses and actually change external reality to fit the preconceived picture you have in your mind. It enables you to continue your illusions and delusions about individuals or groups to fit whatever was imprinted by your culture, despite information which would bring any other observer to a very different, and more accurate, conclusion.

So, both your senses and your culture lead you into illusions, errors, or specific patterns of perceiving. They are built into the structure of your brain/body. They are the way you reconstruct reality to fit into your preconceived and learned modes of understanding.

Many of the errors (or differences) in your perceptions come from these real differences in the biochemistry between you and others. You may get glasses, wear a hearing aide, or train your senses to become increasingly acute, but you can never get them to see exactly what others see. Knowing this should change your mindset.

Instead of angrily and futilely trying to convince others that your perceptions are correct and theirs are wrong, it makes better sense for you and them to try to communicate, appreciate, and understand what you and they are seeing and experiencing.

Deferring judgement goes against the way your brain operates, but you can consciously modify your initial responses by shutting up and taking your time to listen to others. To do this you need to understand just how your ethnocentrism (next chapter) complicates this process.

Thirteen

Ethnocentrism: We Are Better Than You

Whereas egoholism is a "me first, me only" behavior on an individual level, ethnocentrism is "us first, us only" on a group level.

Deep-seated and overwhelming fears are shared by the group. The ethnocentric person or group fears any others who are seen as different. They relieve their fears by making the others comic figures. Laughing at them makes others seem less fearful. Their beliefs and practices are seen as less valuable, less human. The ethnocentric person has learned the behavior expectancies and patterns of his group and these give him security. The others' behaviors are not understandable or are less predictable to him than he would like, which makes him insecure and frightened. If he doesn't know why or what the other is going to do, he is vulnerable to attack which could mean anything from emotional insults and pain to serious injury or death.

Like the musk-oxen who huddle together in a collective circle to protect any member from attack, most humans find strength and protection from their groups. It gives them powers they don't possess on an individual basis. Unfortunately, in doing this they see others outside their groups as unpredictable, uncontrollable -- dangerous.

The same is true with lower animals. Each species, variety, or small group that is formed tends to meet and view any other living animals with fear and suspiciousness until the others have proven themselves nonthreatening. (School clubs, gangs, adult social clubs often show these tendencies.) For the plant-eaters preyed upon by predators it is useful behavior. No creature on earth now can be totally trusting because with man ever present, every animal is in danger of possible extinction.

In prehistoric times when man was nomadic this suspiciousness helped his band of leery men survive the attacks of others. Throughout history man has found it was to his benefit to be fearful and mistrustful of non-tribal members. Even in the recent past to be trusting or unaware of the motives of strangers, or even countrymen who disagreed with your ancestry or politics, was genocidal. The Mayan, Aztecs, West African Blacks, American Indians, European Jews, Cambodians, and all colonial peoples are examples.

77

The Bible and other religious histories of peoples also show that ethnocentrism is deeply rooted in the collective and individual psyche of man. It has been based on realistic fears and its manifestations have actually protected the existence of many groups.

Another positive aspect of ethnocentrism is its creativity. Each group, in its protective cocoon, had to find its own ways to meet the common problems of every group in relation to the stresses, constraints, and unique resources and opportunities of its particular environment. Each met these challenges and created its own customs, clothing, housing, art, music, dance, drama, oral and written language and literature which reflected their collective and individual genius. These, like the behavior patterns of other species, are worthwhile understanding, preserving, and useful to solve future problems. Retaining the pluralism from all the world's ethnic groups increases our genetic pool of solutions. Therefore, we need to encourage the flourishing of individual ethnic groups in the same way we protect endangered species or art from the past.

The sharing with and learning from each group gives everyone additional tools to understand, cope with, and celebrate his humanity. It could be that way -- a curiosity and appreciation of each other's cultures and beliefs, but for most of mankind, they are stuck with the fearful, stimulus-bound, limiting ethnocentrism.

Ethnocentrism is not ethnic pride anymore than egoholism is a legitimate expression of self-confidence and self-esteem. Both are based on fear imbedded in the physiology of the group and individual. Ethnocentrism is the way the group brainwashes or programs each member to believe that its beliefs and practices are the only ones that are correct. Deviation from the groups customs causes severe anxiety, just as conformity to them results in feelings of acceptance and belongingness.

This phenomenon is similar to the compulsions of an obsessive person. As long as he is following his ritual the individual's fears and anxieties are somewhat diminished. If he cannot fulfill these compulsions his fears and anxieties overcome him. The same thing happens with a group member. As long as he follows the beliefs and rituals of his group he feels more secure than when he doesn't. It should be considered that these social imprints or programs are equally as powerful as the DNA/RNA driven genetic codes in determining behavior.

Until you realize and understand how your family, schools and ethnic group have made you into a kind of robot, your alleged freedom of choice is a microcosmic joke played on you.

This does not mean you have to go against everything you've ever been taught. However, to overcome egoholism, you need to think of others and view each as a person. To overcome ethnocentrism you must accept the fact that your group's behaviors are only a small part of the possible, acceptable, and useful behaviors of any group. Belittling others has the same effect as teasing a person. Many of the same dynamics come into play as well as the same results. The person who teases others and dehumanizes them, dehumanizes himself in the process. The same happens when you view another group's behaviors as less effective or important than yours. They and you are dehumanized. If you are more powerful than they are (money, weapons, formal education, etc.), then you probably use the differences as evidence of their inferiority.

In every case of mass murder or genocide, the victor has convinced himself that his victim was somewhat less human (or more subhuman) than he. The kings and aristocracy believed that they were anointed by God to rule the peasants or serfs who, since they had so much less, were less human. The Chinese Communists who imprisoned or killed thousands of their countrymen were convinced their political interpretation of Maoism was more correct than those they killed, imprisoned, or belittled.

Christians in every country have murdered Non-Christians and heretical Christians for not believing in their brand of Christianity. Hindus and Moslems have done the same as well as every other religious group who have had enough members and power to do so. Each was able to use the brain's amazing ability to justify, that is, rationalize behaviors which are logically inconsistent with their professed beliefs. This is called cognitive dissonance -- the ability to hold truly contradictory thoughts and exhibit contradictory behaviors while still holding onto a certain philosophy which seems to be against one of the ideas or behaviors.

The Christian Nazis could systematically annihilate Jews because they had a lifetime of prejudice against them. Given the economic and political conditions of the time, it was easy for Hitler to use the anger and fears of decent Christian people and convince them that the Jews were to blame. In the convoluted thinking of ethnocentrism he equated the differences in cultures to make the Jews less human so they could be killed like dogs in a dog pound.

Remember that there was a bounty on the scalps of Indians just a little over a hundred years ago -- in the United States! In times of black slavery the slaves were captured by other blacks, sold, and transported across the ocean in conditions unfit for animals. The transporting was done by Moslem and Christian businessmen who did not see the slaves as human beings, but objects to be sold. All during slavery, the slaves were treated as useful or prize animals. The healthiest, hardiest were like cattle and their children sold like prime veal. The black businessmen involved in the slave trade also saw those who were weak enough to be captured as less than human.

During the Second World War Americans interned thousands of law-abiding, integrated, Americanized Japanese into camps. They were not criminals nor spies, but their homes and possessions were taken away without any trials during our national panic. During the same time we were fighting the evil Axis powers, blacks were being hunted and hung in the south for being "uppity." Translated that means not playing the fool for morons who were in power.

The same type of thinking goes on today in large corporations or small businesses. Anytime a group decides the fate of one person or thousands of people without their input or consideration of how these decisions will affect them we have a phenomenon that functions like ethnocentrism. Corporate buy-ups in which a plant is closed without phasing the employees out or retraining them is equivalent to treating them as objects. My book about the misuse of power in schools gives many examples of ethnocentric type thinking which dehumanizes people.

The ethnocentrism and prejudice of others also traps the victims of ethnocentrism into self-limiting behaviors. Many Hispanics refuse to learn and use English. Many of the allegedly Special Ed (retarded) children I taught years ago weren't retarded, but were handicapped because one or both of the parents hadn't learned English. The children were unable to compete with English-speaking Hispanics or the children of the ethnic majority.

I have worked with many blacks who refused to modify their speech patterns because it was "giving in." They refused to conform to the middle-class time expectancies which kept them in a constant battle with their teachers, supervisors, or bosses. They blamed these others for prejudice. I told them that I agreed they were right, but asked them what was more important -- getting an education and feeding their families or proving that the whites were ethnocentric and prejudiced?

In my studies of segregation and prejudice I found that most minorities cannot differentiate between those things from their ethnic culture worth salvaging and the socialized patterns and fears which are associated with the subculture of poverty. It is their misreading of these patterns which helps keep them in poverty. I used to tell my black students that I would teach them the speech and behavior patterns which would make it easier for them to get an education and get jobs. I was not asking them to use these in their families, with their friends, or around me. I just wanted them to know what others expected. The choice of using this training was up to them. My students learned how to live more effectively in various worlds.

This is still my message. It is possible to retain the values inherent in whichever ethnic group you belong. If you do not let your fears and ethnocentrism limit you, you can enjoy and benefit from your group, as well as free yourself to appreciate and live with countless others.

It is very difficult for your giant self to emerge when you are fearfully embedded in ethnocentric thinking and patterns.

Fourteen

Either/Or: Battle of Absolutes

As an egoholic ethnocentric your brain and your social imprinting tends to want to organize and classify people, things, or events into simple black or white, up or down, i. e., in either/or categories. This is a direct contradiction of reality as seen by your multiple senses and as it is processed through the sieve of your social imprinting and the idiosyncrasies of your own experiences.

Your child spills his milk. You scream at him that he is stupid. He attaches the label to himself, not the particular act. You and he generalize that label, stupid, and he believes that he is stupid in everything. In his mind either he is stupid or he's smart. Repeated enough times in an emotional context (which means that many more parts of the brain/body are making permanent memory imprints) he only believes his stupidity more and more. He becomes the victim of your and his either/or thinking.

Marie looks as beautiful to me when she awakes as she did when she went to bed. Yet, there are times when she looks ordinary. Either she's beautiful or she's ordinary? No, the degree of her beauty is dependent upon many factors such as amount of sleep, the foods she's been eating, care of her shin, amount and type of make-up, and her emotional state of mind. It also depends on the state of my libido. The times when my sex drive peaks she is the beautiful dancer/model I met a quarter century ago. When it's low, she looks attractive, but I see our grandchildren's grandma. Either she's beautiful or she isn't? No, it's a matter of degree and dependent on many factors controlled by her as well as many other factors that influence the eye of the beholder.

You read about a murderer. Is he good or bad? Obviously he's bad, an evil person. When you read about his life you find he led an exemplary life. He was considered kind, thoughtful, even a loving Christian man by his family and neighbors. Your opinion changes. You read that he killed his father who was a minister. Your opinion changes towards evil. You find that his father had abused his wife and family for twenty years. His father was kicking his mother when the murderer snapped, and, in a blind rage killed his father. Is the killer good or bad? To me he was a reasonably good man who committed a horrendous act. To the extremists he would still be either a murderer (bad) or an overly stressed man (good).

Clarence Darrow brought shadings of guilt, evil, and good into the courtrooms when he proved that even murderers have mitigating circumstances that should be considered before judgement is passed. He was making a case against simplistic either/or thinking.

Many people say that if their mate were ever unfaithful that would be the end of their marriage. They tell everyone they would get a divorce. A man discovers his mate is cheating. He had assumed that if she cheated it was because she no longer loved him. She still does love him, but he is trapped in his either/or thinking and has to uphold his previous statements about what he would do if this infidelity ever happened. He refuses to listen to her, to understand the shadings, the reasons for her actions, and sees the event in black or white terms. He gets a divorce and loses a person who loves him deeply and whom he loves.

I have been extremely successful with most of the children I've taught, especially those who had been negatively labeled as retarded, stupid, hyperactive, lazy, and hostile. I seldom read their records nor paid any attention to the labels their parents or teachers applied to them. I refused to use either/or thinking. Instead, I assumed these children had done things that disturbed others because of how they had been treated and the type of environment in which the disturbance occurred. As a result of being treated with respect and having their environments modified, most of the children quickly made miraculous (to the parents, teachers) changes for the better.

How did I manage to escape the trap of either/or thinking? As a child I went to over a dozen schools in three states before I graduated from high school. I came into each neighborhood quietly, minded my own business, and quickly became accepted. I was welcomed into my new friends' homes and their parents were accepting and friendly -- until they discovered I was Jewish. Many fellow students were not allowed to associate with me and on a few occasions my new girl friends were forced to stop dating me. I was the same person before and after the label, but not to prejudiced people. Either I was a good (Christian) person or a bad (Jewish) one.

It was a painful, but eventually a liberating experience because I have spent most of my life trying to understand why people mistreat each other. I still think in either/or terms. As I've said, either/or thinking is built into the wiring of your brain and nervous system and our social customs reflect this wiring. That is, it's part of the way social institutions operate. Knowing this, I try to think before I respond and consciously examine my intended response to see whether it is either/or.

This technique works especially well in my dealings with my students because I seldom express my initial reactions, but decide what to do or say after I've filtered out my self-preservation, socially imprinted responses and then use whatever I think will best serve the student's needs.

The technique of counting to ten before speaking is very helpful only if you also do this. Examine your gut level feelings, accept them, let them pass, then carefully think of as many different scenarios and consequences as you can from each of your possible statements or actions; then choose the one which best serves you and the other person.

You will gradually find it easier and easier to defer your initial either/or thinking and judgements and the quality of your decisions will markedly improve because you are operating in your giant self mode. The other way you and your victims are always diminished, dehumanized.

Fifteen

Personalizing: Normal Paranoia

When someone says to you, "Now, don't take this personally!" there's almost a certainty that;

1) it is meant to be taken personally,
2) you will take it personally, and
3) it will be painful to you.

This chapter is not about this phenomenon. When someone is consciously, purposely, addressing a suggestion or criticism to you then it is meant for you to take it personally. How you react to this criticism is modified by who the person is, his power over you, the setting it takes place in, and the actual worth of his criticism.

This chapter is about the things that are not directed at you, the bullet that doesn't have your name on it, but which you jump into and which buries itself in your heart and mind. This chapter is about your distortion of innocent statements or actions or even hostile remarks or behaviors overheard, but not directed at you.

Example: After being rejected because I was Jewish, I became sensitive to the word. I can remember my stomach tying up in knots if someone offered me "Orange Juice." I was paranoid, so sensitive, so constantly on guard against real or imagined slights that instead of "juice" I heard "Jewish". It's funny now, but then it made my life a nightmare about to happen.

In comparative animal studies it was found that most of the things humans can do animals can do also, but not as well, especially the higher mental processes. There is both a quantitative and qualitative difference between animal and human behavior. There are shades of differences. The same holds true between the behavior of a very disturbed person classified as a paranoid and normal behavior when you are personalizing statements or events.

The paranoid believes that almost everything that happens relates to something he has done or said. His behavior is the extreme in personalizing. A casual look from a stranger and he's certain he is being spied on. A conversation nearby may be sufficient evidence to convince him that those people are talking about him. Local, state, or international politics are filled with events that he is sure are being created to make his life personally difficult and dangerous.

Everyone believes such things to some degree because the events happening elsewhere do affect all of us. The difference is that normal people don't believe these events are happening just to hurt or inconvenience them personally.

Paranoid behavior is normal distrust and healthy suspiciousness concerning the motives of others taken to a crippling extreme. The paranoid is an either/or thinker and cannot discriminate the shadings, the reality of a situation. A totally mature and healthy person (if she/he existed) would be able to discern whether others' actions were directed towards him or not and the degree to which they were. Most people can see these shadings. On bad days or during angry or depressive moments healthy people more easily place negative loadings on events not personally directed at them. Paranoids are always having a bad day.

If you are planning a picnic and it rains you have many ways to interpret and cope with your disappointment. If you recognize that weather prediction is still an inexact science and you don't blame anyone, but change your plans accordingly, you're quite healthy. If you believe God changed the weather to inconvenience you that is childish egoholism. You are saying that everything, even a natural phenomenon, revolves around you and your needs. Actually, you feel powerless and this is a compensatory mechanism to make you feel more powerful -- which is what paranoids do. If you think a real or alleged enemy conjured up the weather just to hurt you, you're in deep _____!

In any situation in which human error causes an accident, that wasn't premeditated or intentional but results in damage or harm, the paranoid sees the accident as intentional or planned. The more you lose your emotional distance and objectivity, the easier it is to personalize an accidental occurrence.

It is not healthy to be so objective that you become cold and devoid of feeling. This just avoids the pains of human emotions and conflicts. Expressions of your emotions are often healthy, even appropriate. If your car is hit you are not expected to act in a mechanical, zombie manner. However, remember that the other person is also in the throes of confusion and heightened feelings too.

As your children get older you lose more and more absolute control over them. You need to modify your behavior if you want them to love and respect you. Your child stays out late. He is out because he is enjoying himself and he loses track of time. You are fearful and worried. Maybe you think he is staying out just to make you worry and to disobey your wishes. The discrepancy between reality and your fears is the result of your personalizing his behavior.

My daughter, Arrianne, used to remove the neck rest when she used my car. She usually forgot to replace it. I hovered between paranoia and personalizing because I began to think she did it hostilely. I told her several times to put it back, but when she continued doing it I felt rejected, hurt, unloved, finally very angry. When I explained how she was making me feel, plus not letting her use the car for a week, she always put it back where it belonged.

There was a big difference between what I personalized and reality. I had assumed hostility, but it was thoughtlessness. If I hadn't told her my perceptions and she had not apologized, I would have continued to wrongly personalize her intentions.

Whenever a school principal came up with an idea that interfered with my program my gut level reaction was paranoia. I read malevolence, an effort to stifle my creativity. Now, I wait for my reactions to pass because I know I'm personalizing. His promoting his own ideas may well be a way for him to get me to do things as he sees fit, which is his legal right. I no longer see it as a conscious act to anger me. I try to see his directive from his point of view. This is a general antidote for personalizing. If I still disagree I have a private conference with him to air any differences as I attempt to grasp his reality and get him to see mine.

At times I will see the value of the principal's input and change my program. If I still feel his ideas will have an adverse effect I explain why. Since neither of us is attacking, but trying to understand the other's views and mutually exploring options, we can listen and modify our positions without feeling we have been manipulated. With few exceptions compromises are made which allow us to save face, i.e., retain our professional integrity and opinions while modifying our positions.

This type of exchange in education is very unusual. I earned this right by fighting for my share of the power. With enough appropriate and legal power it is easier not to get trapped in personalizing situations. No one in power is going to give it to you so there are real risks involved. I paid my dues for what I have.

When I first met Marie I spent night and day with her. I knew her like a book. After we had been married a few years and we had yours, mine, and ours living with us I couldn't study her as I had done. We would get into arguments and I'd ask her what was bugging her. She would tell me that I knew what it was -- but I didn't. Finally, I told her I was not a mind-reader and either she had to explain to me what was bothering her or I would leave. She had been personalizing my actions. She had read many of my actions as intentionally hostile and neglectful. I felt I was spending the most time I could with her and still do my school job, my extra job, and have time for the family. Instead of sharing her concerns and telling me what bothered her she wanted me to take the time to study her to figure out what she needed or wanted. Once she stopped personalizing, taking my actions as rejection, she was able to cope with the time problem and I was better able to meet more of her needs.

When we personalize now, the victim usually helps the other get his/her sense of perspective. She/He stops, thinks, and we are able to discuss the situation. It does not always work (usually because of some unfinished business which has been awakened) or does not work immediately because it is common in our culture to personalize. After all, it is you who are feeling the effects of the event. Your perception of the event is reality because it feels and is real! Yet, it is also a distortion of the event, an error of perception, a misreading of the other's intentions.

You personalize because the other person has done or said something and within your body you feel some real pain, hurt, and/or anger. The crucial questions are did the other person intentionally mean to cause you pain? Was it deserved, that is, was it a legitimate and accurate assessment of you and an event, but still a poorly handled criticism? Was it some problem, like unfinished business in his past, and is he using you as a scapegoat?

With a paranoid almost everything is reorganized so that he feels most situations reflect the evil intentions of others which cause him pain and discomfort. He can't tell his friends from his enemies.

Personalizing causes you to feel pain and to misinterpret the event. Unlike a paranoid you don't experience this with everyone, but selectively. The task is to understand why this person rings your bell. Usually, he is in a position to make your life uncomfortable and you believe you are powerless to say or do what you feel is necessary. At this point you must evaluate whether he owns the problem or you are misinterpreting it. If it is you, then you need to reevaluate honestly what you can do. If it is him, then you have to be courageous and determine your trade-off in confronting him.

Since no one is so secure and mature that he always evaluates every situation accurately and realistically and then determines his and the others' responsibilities and rights, it is a reasonable assumption that you tend to personalize most situations. Once you can admit and see personalizing as a constant source of error, you can act rather than react. This means checking your tendency towards taking each action or statement personally and reacting from gut level feelings. Instead it means listening with your heart and mind, asking questions to determine the intentions of the other, and constantly reassessing the event until you have managed to achieve a livable compromise or balance with your believed attacker.

I reiterate, if you have done the above and the other is intentionally attacking you, then it is not personalizing, it is a personal affront and you need to confront or deal with him using your strengths. If he has valid cause but you are in pain, then you still can demand humane criticism.

Remember, personalizing is a part of your evolutionary history, a heightened bodily awareness of attack, and is wired into your brain. Moreover, your social imprinting distorts it further. You always will have the tendency to personalize, but the more aware you are of this tendency, the easier it will be for you to control it rather than it controlling you.

Sixteen

Possessiveness: Who Owns Whom, and Why?

Possessiveness is rooted in fear. The possessor is afraid the person or object (often seen as the same) is going to be lost, taken away, or leave. The possessor is operating on the basis of his diminished self.

Possessiveness also is physiological. It is rooted in a male's brain-body from his evolutionary history when one male was the possessor of a small band of females, children, and subordinate males. Learning to be nonpossessive is important as individual and family roles are being redefined in the light of present and future needs. However, it is not easy to overcome a survival pattern which is embedded in the brain/body of every human. If our species doesn't learn, doesn't develop new ways of relating without possessiveness, it may destroy itself.

Slavery is the possession of one person by another. It is usually legally sanctioned by a society and severely limits the freedom of the possessed. Slavery based on race legally ended in the U.S.A. with the Emancipation Proclamation. Gender slavery ended with women getting the vote in the 20th Century. Man's conditioning about a woman's "place" is still being fought in the marketplace, institutions, and in the bedroom. Child slavery still continues, but has been lessened by laws enunciating and protecting their rights. Economic slavery remains a reality for most Americans and most working people throughout the world. If you are at the mercy of a boss or job, are in debt, just barely make it month to month, then you're an economic slave.

Women have been men's property throughout Western history. It was her duty to satisfy her husband's sexual needs, care for children, forage for food, work the land, and do what her master decreed. He protected her from other males and dangers, and fulfilled her basic needs.

In the long history of families it has been only in the past few centuries that love between a male and female was possible or even a consideration, except for the privileged few who had the time for it. The process of falling in love and courting is very time and energy consuming. The average working person neither had the time nor the energy to do it. Romantic love for the common folk as portrayed in the movies has been possible recently because so many more people have the money and leisure time to pursue its ephemeral delights.

In the past if a woman and man loved one another that was a pleasant bonus, it was not something required or expected. A man's word was the law. His physical and legal strengths were the reality. He owned his wife (wives) and children in exactly the same way he owned (possessed) his other things (property). Anything on his property, territory, was his to do with as he pleased. He could whip, beat, even kill his animals, wives, and children with relative impunity because he owned them. Other men did not want the law dictating how they should use or abuse their property-territory so there was social collusion against the possessed. The same state of affairs existed in the relations between workers and bosses which is why the union movement grew so strong during this century.

We are frightened by the powers of youth gangs and their territorial needs, but their behavior appears to be the way of our species. Whether this behavior is mainly biological, sociological or an interaction between them, it is a reality. Think of gangs as roving bands of subordinate males, gathering strength by their numbers in order to get their share of the limited resources available in their environments.

From childhood on you are taught not to touch another person without his/her permission. It is considered an invasion of space-territory. The concept of personal, private space has expanded and is treated like any other possession. It is divided and owned. Look what happens in crowds. Each protects his private space in an effort to exercise his individuality and not be overwhelmed. Concern with private space would often be funny if it didn't cause so much anxiety.

Socialism and communism have tried to convince people that property belongs to the state, not to any individual. Buddhism teaches that the concepts of property and possessiveness are what causes pain and suffering. It teaches its adherents not to be involved in the pursuit of things because they are all temporary as are the pleasures they bring. Buddhist teaching implies much more than this negativity as it replaces the temporary with the permanence of the spiritual. Possibly, such ideologies developed because of the abuses of possessiveness.

Group marriages, communes, spouse swapping, and open marriages are examples of individuals and groups who believe that the concept of property with its resultant possessiveness and insane jealousies were inappropriate and damaging. Most of these alternatives, however, haven't been successful. Part of the reason is they had to exist within hostile environments which insured their failure.

As individual liberties have increased here and worldwide, more people are challenging the limitations placed upon them by property laws. New laws give minorities, handicapped, wives, and children rights so they cannot be physically or emotionally abused and injured. Even a woman's former "duty" to have sex with her husband has been challenged. Sex has to be mutual, because if he forces her it may be construed as rape. Children can sue their parents. These last two types of cases are difficult to win, but they show how society is changing. More and more human dignity and freedom are being supported by law.

The concept of consenting adults means that your body is yours. No one can buy or use it through marriage or any other type of contract without your consent. It belongs to you, no matter what your age, sex, or ethnicity. (The reality of economics and various degrees of personal dependency modifies this in reality, but not in principle.)

If you do not belong to anyone, you are free. But, this also means that so is everyone else, so no one can possess another. Those involved in the new freedoms have found there are some wrenching trade-offs which cause new problems, choices, and responsibilities. Some of the trade-offs seem worse than the problems they were supposed to cure. (Eden was security. The apple is filled with worms and choices.) To be responsible for all of your choices is a fearsome burden. You have to accept the blame and the consequences of your choices. It means learning from your errors or repeating them in a repetitious process of pain. For many people such freedom is not worth it. As Erich Fromm wrote, most people want to escape from freedom and welcome the security of their bondage. They would rather have a master who is responsible for their welfare and who they can blame and hate when things go wrong. Uncertainty, insecurity, and loneliness seem too heavy a price to pay for increased freedom. Your diminished self is comforted by other diminished selves, but your giant self seems to often stand alone. (Maybe you would be happier destroying this book, it may be safer, more comforting.)

Before the new freedoms, before the idea that your mind/body belonged to you, when you married you expected the marriage to last a lifetime. Certainly you gave up variety, much of your freedom, but the security and stability were worth it. You knew your spouse might cheat, but if he did he paid a heavy price socially, psychologically, ethically, religiously, and financially. There were many sanctions to make certain that each of you deeply believed and accepted the sentence of "till death do us part." (Of course, the reprieve of death came earlier then, but now, with life extension, you could spend one hundred years with the same wrinkled face staring at you while sharing your bowls of oatmeal.)

Growing freedom means more difficult choices. If you own your mind/body/soul, why can't you share it with whomever you wish without your partner becoming frightened, hurt, or angry. You can, but the same freedom must be given to your partner or spouse. The question is, can humans, tied to their evolutionary genetic survival patterns and the learned social ones, overcome their fear-based possessiveness?

Many spouses cannot stand their mates doing anything without them. Some could handle a night out with members of the same sex as long as the mate didn't fraternize with the opposite sex. Some can allow their spouses to do anything with anyone else if it doesn't take away from their relationship and doesn't involve a sexual relationship. They have a legitimate point because sex can be tied to such powerful bodily reactions and emotions that it could destroy their ongoing relationship. Others go places that they hate with their spouses, but do because they're afraid to leave their spouses alone. Why? Because in an open, free environment, their spouse might find someone more interesting, more intelligent, or more attractive. This could result in the loss of the spouse, the Primary Person who means stability and security.

I can understand why so many women still feel this insecurity. Despite the improvements, most women do not receive equal pay for equal work nor can they as easily compete in the marketplace because it remains a man's world. Further, women are still the primary caregivers and the ones expected to raise the children. For true sexual freedom, for insane possessiveness to end or be minimized, women's rights must be legally, socially, and in actual practice equal to men's. As it now stands, in open competition for mates and companions for various reasons, women are much more vulnerable than men. Voters who want the freedoms a nonpossessive world would bring need to push their legislators to pass laws that would enable women to compete equally. As importantly, men and women need to change their mindset.

The heart of jealously-possessiveness is not love, but cold, naked fear. You are afraid of losing what you think you possess. Many laws and customs are efforts of the average man who needs protection against the predations of the extraordinary man. The extraordinary man usually is able, like the dominant male of any animal pack, to get more than his share of whatever is considered desirable. Without laws and ethical-social sanctions, polygamy or polyandry would be more common and the extraordinary man or woman would have much more of everything and many of the average people would have very little.

Despite man-made rules, some people still possess more than others. I don't foresee this changing, no matter what kinds of social structures are developed. Whatever laws or customs are created, some people will use them to meet their real and believed needs. Since each person is unique, those who can best gain access to those traits, skills, or abilities which express their giant selves will get more of whatever they need or want than those who operate from their diminished selves.

We opted out of the Garden of Eden where we were innocent (stupid?). There is no way to have it all. If you're a person who values protection and security and you are willing to be dependent upon another person, then you probably want to be possessed by another and want to possess him/her. If you want the freedom to discover and expand the boundaries of your giant self and find being possessed and possessing limiting, then you will lose a sense of security and stability.

The important thing to decide, a decision which is an expression of your giant self, is what you want and can live with. I drew extremes; most people live within various gradations. I've tried to explain the evolutionary and social forces acting upon you, but when push comes to shove, you still have choices. These choices each have specific consequences, many of which are quite predictable. Some are not. Very few choices are carved in stone. If you make a mistake or don't like a consequence, you can make a different choice. This is the beauty of escaping from Eden. But, don't whine about the consequences. Uncertainty and pain are the trade-offs of choice -- and the ecstatic pleasures and manifest the joys of an expanding consciousness.

If possessiveness is a built-in biochemical program like thirst and hunger, then very little can be done. If a man's possessiveness is due to the amount of testosterone, estrogen, and progesterone in his bloodstream then it can be modified by altering his hormones. I think that man is quite flexible and malleable. He is shaped by his genetics and social imprintings. However, more than any other animal he can understand these forces and, through his will and choices change his internal and external environments in ways to recreate himself and his species.

So, choose to be possessed or possessive, but admit to yourself what you are choosing and accept the consequences. The same holds for those who don't wish to possess or be possessed. Recognize the trade-offs, make your choices in the daylight of knowledge and be prepared for the joys and sorrows of these decisions.

Seventeen

Scientific Error: Errors of Great Magnitude

Before the Scientific Revolution men asked, "What happens when you come to the edge of the world, do you fall off?" The question was based on the physical observation and assumption that the world was flat. Men assumed that what their senses told them was unquestionably true. (Remember how your senses lie). So they began with an erroneous assumption based on observation which led to the incorrect question resulting in the wrong answer.

In science as in life, the question will determine the answer. The narrower the question the narrower the answer. The greatest discoveries come from the best questions. Take a mundane example. A pencil is missing. You ask Bill if he took it. He can honestly say he didn't. If you had asked him where go got it, he may have told you from Janet who actually stole it.

The process of interrogation or asking the right questions in one mastered by the best lawyers, police, teachers, scientists, business men, and suspicious spouses. In science and industry it has been proven that well constructed questions elicit more discoveries than the best answers. Many times a problem which is defying a solution is easily answered once the questioner poses the question differently.

In personal relationships the questions you ask often are not constructed to give the answers you need. "Will you love me forever?", shows your insecurity and fears and places a burden on the other person. A better question, that is, one in which you have greater input and control would be, "What do I need to do that will keep our love alive?"

The first question cannot be answered except hypothetically. The second can be answered very specifically and productively. The first would lead to mutual confusion, fear, and guilt, whereas the second would lead to productive, open discussions, understanding, and constructive actions.

"Does God exist?" This is a question about an infinite entity that cannot be grasped intellectually by any questioner because humans are finite. Better questions would be, "If God exists what is expected of me? If God doesn't exist what should be the basis of human ethics? Where do I get my strength to live in a fearful and uncertain world? Without God what is the meaning of life?"

The structure of the question will determine the form of the answer. The more clearly you pose the question, the clearer you are about what you want to know, the more specific and clear will be your answer. Every question will have its advantages and disadvantages. Every question will have limitations which will result in limitations in your answer. Be aware that the way you phrase your question will lead you towards some kinds of answers and away from others. Some errors will be the inevitable results.

For many people science has replaced God, religion, and faith because it seems to be able to explain and prove its various positions and beliefs logically and rationally. Science has resulted in greatly increased knowledge, more creature comforts, and is a healthy balance to wild superstition. But, science and scientists are fallible, are liable to many types of errors, such as erroneous assumptions and wrong questions.

A major type of error is the belief in an objective observer. Most research is based on the belief that the scientist can be unbiased, a totally objective observer. He believes because of his training and knowledge that he can observe objects, events, people, or themselves without subjective influences. Actually, it is impossible to be a totally objective observer. All the types of errors I've been explaining are all human and most of them unavoidable because of the nature of our brains/bodies. Scientists make these types of errors too. Those that understand that they make these and other unconscious errors find ways to compensate for them. They use methods such as statistical analyses, double-blind experiments, and review by people with nothing to gain from the research. Those who arrogantly claim objectivity usually commit numerous errors which they impose upon an unsuspecting public.

Since the scientist and his observations are subject to error, scientific conclusions must be suspect, especially initially, before they have been subjected to review. This does not mean that the scientist's research, observations, and conclusions are invalid, just that you need to be cautious about accepting them without question. In fact, most scientists welcome intelligent questioning. It gives them the chance to further think through their conclusions, explain them, and to determine next steps. They admit that no experiment is free from errors or contaminations. By admitting this, they can then repeat the experiments, change them to fit new data, encourage others to duplicate them, and then couch their findings in terms like "it appears," "it seems like," or "it is indicated."

Many times a researcher will find that when others duplicate his experiments they get different results. Dr. Roger Williams was attacked. Years later he discovered that one group of his attackers had used a different form of B3. He found that they had used a less expensive form of the vitamin and one that didn't contain the amide molecule which would have made a difference. He assumed they knew the difference so he hadn't thought of that as a reason their experiments failed.

In the controversy over vitamin C, most of the experimenters didn't use near the dosage Dr. Linus Pauling used, yet they blasted his results and insulted him when they didn't get the same results. In fact, most did the experiments to prove him wrong. They brought their biases with them, didn't follow his experimental design, and changed the dosages which were the basis of his claim, and then had the "objectivity" to say he was a fraud. So much for scientific objectivity.

Most social scientists have been intimidated by the observer effect. The hard science of physics allegedly was above this problem. Atomic particles were supposed to all follow natural, known laws; that is, they were predictable. Heisenberg's Indeterminancy Principle was the beginning of the end for this idea. He found that if you knew where a particle was located, you couldn't accurately determine its velocity. If you knew its velocity, you couldn't be certain where it was. You could know one, but not both. Recently, particles such as the cobalt atom and even subatomic particles seem to make "choices." That is, the scientists predict the particle will go in a specific direction as it has before, but while being "observed" it behaves differently. So physics, the science others are based upon, suffers from the "observer effect."

Social scientists are still defensive because of the enormous number of uncontrolled and uncontrollable variables with affect their research. Psychologists could easily see how anthropologists were unable to be objective about the people they were studying because the anthropologists' own cultural values were imprinted in them so that they could not see reality in the framework of the primitives. Even the label "primitives" which they gave the natives was itself a cultural judgement proving their built-in bias.

The anthropologists could smile at the naivete of the psychologists who believed that they could be objective in dealing with their clients. I supervised an ex-divinity student who was a psychologist. I can remember hearing his excited footsteps as he ran through the hall to my office to report the latest bizarre sexual experiences told to him by one of his psychotic patients. The patients had quickly learned that to get the most attention from him they needed to tell him graphic sexual exploits. He was not an objective observer, but he was a kind, caring person who did help his patients. I was able to help him realize what they were doing, which helped his growth and their improvement.

Since total objectivity is impossible in any science, it is unsafe to base any judgements on a single finding or test. Yet, non-scientists do it frequently. In my district when proficiency tests were mandated by the state it was decided that they were to be the sole determinant of whether a child passed to the next grade. There were many complex reasons for this decision and it was based on the judgement of very qualified educators. I tried to explain that the tests used were neither scientifically valid nor reliable. That objectivity is not perfect nor totally possible and is always liable to error, does not mean that it is not a worthwhile goal and a scientific tool but it must be tempered by compassion.

Logic is another scientific tool. In logic specific facts, rules of evidence and proof are used to arrive at a conclusion. It is a healthy improvement over hasty decisions made by the wiring, superstitions, and prejudices left over from our previous evolution. Logic claims to be objective (heard that before?). It is based on beginning with a specific premise believed to be correct and subsequent statements and arguments leading to proof. Even if the premise is wrong, the forcefulness of the logical method can make the result appear correct when it isn't. All the facts, all the arguments leading from the premise to the proof are taken from an infinite number of possibilities and each is selected by a human. Use logic because it is a useful instrument, but be aware how you use it and how it is used on you.

Probability and statistics: Since scientists each see, organize, and interpret reality somewhat differently, which leads to many kinds of errors, they need some way of averaging, a means to reach a compromise or consensus about what is "out there."

Probability: If enough people are quizzed about what they see and experience then the range of all their responses should give us a picture of reality. It is difficult to talk about the whole range of responses so scientists take the sum of these and get an average. They know that this average doesn't perfectly describe what every person saw, but it does indicate a consensual reality. Each person would vary from the average. Scientists know there will be errors and that these errors can be statistically predicted.

Statisticians admit there is error in every type of measurement. They expect and can predict the amount of error. What will determine the degree of error is the size of the sample population, the inherent accuracy of the data collected, and the statistical methods used. Imagine that! Science does not say it's perfectly correct, but instead refers you to the amount of error involved. Again, error is expected. By using probability theory, statistics, and good experimental designs errors are not eliminated, but are categorized and minimized. Think of it. Few scientists will consider an experiment or take a theory seriously that can not be analyzed using some sort of statistical procedures. Yet, these all begin with the assumption of built-in error.

The very foundations of science are based on this important premise. The methodology of science, that is, the attitudes towards objective and subjective observations, suspended judgement, carefully controlled experimentation, replicability, and statistical verification are all aids in helping us understand and evaluate the world. It is the scientific methodology which is the expression of an attitude towards understanding phenomena which is important, not any of its factors. Even though it leads to many kinds of errors, the scientific method is still a healthy basis for overcoming the impulsivity of genetic and social imprints.

Interestingly enough, the quality of thought or practice held most in disrepute by the average scientist is intuition. Yet, intuition is the one mode most often identified by the greatest scientists as that which helped them in their discoveries.

Intuition is a legitimate mode of thinking/feeling, but is also subject to errors. Intuition is a felt sense that something is true, real, or correct, but it is considered to be too subjective and unscientific. I would agree that it is and has been a major source of human error. It is difficult to differentiate between what you want to believe is true and what is true, because you want to believe something so badly that you do feel it to be the truth. Therefore, I would not want to encourage you to believe in intuition as your main way of knowing or understanding. It is very easy to delude yourself. In this respect the attitude of the scientist, despite his errors, is superior to a misguided trust in your intuition alone.

In the hands of a person who is knowledgeable in a field, knows how to use the scientific method, there often occurs an intuitive feeling/thought that defies logic or rationality, but leads to a solution to a problem or provides a new insight. Intuition often occurs to artists and scientists as a feeling that something fits, is right. Every major innovator I've met or read about has had this experience. Intuition is more than just some magical, inexplicable happening, but rather is a synthesis of prior knowledge, a felt sense, followed by a cognitive reorganization. The latter, in the form of a conscious, rational, logical explanation surfaces to make it easier for others to understand and share.

My first conscious awareness of this was as a struggling novelist. Each time after I thought I had found my style I would reread the work and find it stupid and amateurish. One night, while writing about my father's death many years earlier, I seemed to lift off, leave my awareness of where I was as I became totally absorbed. I cried as I wrote and knew that, no matter what anyone said, I was finally a creative writer. (My intuition may have been correct, but editors/publishers didn't agree.)

As a young teacher I had deep feelings about certain things I was trying and a felt revulsion about the hypocrisy of schooling. Since I couldn't explain nor rationally defend my experiments and concepts I was told to stop. I persisted even thought I knew I was endangering my career. Gradually I worked out the bugs, read voraciously, and then was able to defend my practices. I even gathered statistical and anecdotal evidence to prove and verify my premises. However, some of my gut level intuitions were wrong. Like any other type of incoming information, intuitions can be wrong.

I am an enthusiastic supporter of science even though it is filled with possibilities for error. In the proper hands both the scientific method and intuition are powerful tools for knowing. As long as you realize that any method, properly learned and applied can give only part of any answer, some of the truth, then you can learn to use a variety of methods with increasing sophistication and success.

The problem of believing science or scientists is the problem of blindly believing any expert or authority. In science eminence and authority is usually earned by research, thoughtfulness, questions, or innovations in a discipline. Prestige in a discipline has usually been accomplished through a single-minded devotion to one train of thought and the exclusion of others, including equally valuable solutions to the same problem(s). The fame that comes with discovery tends to keep the scientist tied to a technique, concept, or idea and actually limits him from considering new options or directions. What he has conceptualized as a truth can be proven, demonstrated, and logically defended using scientific tools. Yet his eminence and fame may blind him to the inevitable errors inherent in a system or to other equally valid solutions.

Because scientists are human and vulnerable to the same errors as other humans, you must beware of blindly accepting their solutions. What an individual scientist has created and believes may be of great use and service to you, to many others, or be found to be worthless. My caution to you is to carefully examine the scientist's background (to understand his reality), premises, design and methods or research, validity and reliability of his statistical methods (if statistics are relevant to his theory), and the part intuition or other types of knowing played in his thinking. Then determine the advantages and disadvantages of his conclusions to you. This suggested evaluation says nothing about the alleged truth or accuracy of a scientist's work, but how it fits into your pictures of reality.

This does not mean that you throw a scientific finding out because it doesn't fit into your previous bias or limited view of reality. A new idea may well be correct, worthwhile, and benefit you -- if you give it the chance. That's why, after you have made a conscious choice and accepted the possibility it may have value for you, you need to bring the scientist's belief system, his new reality into yours. However, it after giving it your best shot and it doesn't work for you, don't immediately blame the authority or yourself. This scientist's work may not be for you, there may not be a good fit, and no one is at fault.

Still, it may be that you didn't understand nor were you willing to accept a scientist's idea because it might have meant you would have to make major adjustments in your thinking and feeling or your behavior. (Some of the ideas I will share later will probably scare, anger, and disgust some of you while they will delight, amuse, or stimulate others.) Your rejection of a scientific finding may well be your fault, your diminished self being unable to deal with new information.

Or, the "authority" in question may well be a false guru, a bad scientist but an excellent publicist. He may be a con-man, or a charismatic person who manages to create changes by virtue of his charm and personality, but whose ideas are unable to be successfully used by others. The latter type of scientific figure doesn't realize this and sometimes can be dangerous because he cannot understand why others can't do what comes easily to him. He doesn't mean to, but he makes others feel inadequate and failures. I'm telling you not to let him, the others, or their disciples convince you it's all your fault if you don't understand or succeed in their realities. No system, no theory, no technique, and no scientist has answers or solutions that are applicable to everyone, even though the most popular and powerful authorities try to convince you that if you follow their directions and then fail in their systems, it's all your fault. Nonsense!

As an authority in several fields I feel that I can help many people. Obviously this is one of the reasons I'm writing this book. I have been a charismatic teacher who was successful and watched angrily as others who imitated me totally misinterpreted and abused my ideas. I anguished over why and came up with ways to more effectively help teachers who are willing to devote the courage and energy necessary to attain the flexibility to be successful. I have seen how effective my ideas are which is the reason for my self-confidence.

Any authority has to believe deeply in himself or no one will believe or follow him. He has to believe he is right and has answers. You don't!!! You should use authorities in the same way you should use science -- as a means of understanding multiple realities. Some of the ideas of these authorities will be perfect fits for you. Some may be difficult and hazardous, but worth the effort. Some are wrong for you, but right for others. Some are wrong. Some are even deliberate scams and lies.

Although carefully examining the authority as I suggested will help, anyone who tells you it is easy to know which one is to be trusted and which one is not is a fool or a liar.

Eighteen

Triune Brain: Simultaneous Messages

Evolution seems to point to a three-part or triune brain in humans. In Paul MacLean's model, the brain is an entity in three concentric layers. Each layer is a physical reality and a metaphor for functions. The most primitive, earliest layer is the brain stem, often called the reptilian brain because it is part of all vertebrates form the reptile to man. It is the part that regulates the vital body functions of heart beat and respiration. These were considered to be entirely involuntary as were other systems of the body. That is, as with other animals, these functions did not necessitate consciousness. They were automatic, involuntary because they were too important to depend on conscious control. These were functions, which if they didn't work, could end the animal's life in seconds or minutes. When animals' lives were in danger they didn't have the luxury of cogitating upon all the ramifications of their actions. An immediate response came from the reptilian brain. Now it is believed that with training and conscious will, these reptilian responses and functions can be controlled, at least modified in intensity.

The next evolutionary addition was the limbic system or mammalian brain. It is difficult to simplify all that it does because it interacts with so many other parts of the brain/body simultaneously. The metaphor of the feeling brain gives you the flavor, the emotion of its function. Think of it as the center of your emotional life. It is deeply affected by the impulses and messages of the reptilian brain. Through interactions from the pituitary gland and the hypothalamus your sexual feelings, anger, rage, love, reverence, hate, fear, and other emotions and emotional shadings occur. The hypothalamus controls your appestat which affects your appetite for food as well as your thirst-regulating mechanisms. All these functions do not occur in isolation, but are complex bio-chemical-electrical happenings interacting with many systems of the body simultaneously.

The next layer, the convoluted grayish portion, the neocortex, the cerebrum, is the center for the organization and direction of all the higher mental processes. This portion of the brain could be considered the center of consciousness, although much more is involved in consciousness than just the cortex. Although it appears that as you ascend the evolutionary scale many animals have increasing degrees of consciousness, in man the functioning of consciousness is most highly developed. The sophisticated abilities to use symbols, create languages, create and use tools, as well as reasoning abilities all stem from the neocortex's interactions with other parts of the brain/body simultaneously.

I will take liberties with Freud's three part system of the id, ego, and superego, but metaphorically they may help our understanding of the brain. Think of the id as the ultimate source of your primitive, survival drives. It is necessary for your basic needs. It is your personal life support and species survival system.

Your ego gives you further impetus for self-preservation, but it includes the development of the conception that you are unique, different from other humans and objects in your environment. It is the part that makes you emotionally aware that there is a you that is different and separate from others and the ego is going to get your needs met, even at the expense for others. It is the self, the emotional feeling of I-ness. Very loosely it is like the mammalian, the limbic brain. Egotism, means you think of yourself first. Egotism is evolutionary self-preservation. Like the reptilian brain it is not good or bad, it just is.

The superego, sometimes explained as the conscience, is the you that is sensitive to, aware of, imprinted and controlled by others and by the institutions in your environment. It is consciousness taken to the level of other-centeredness, rather than egotistic self-centeredness. The superego can lead to the highest levels of sociological, ecological, and cosmic development. Or, it can be used for maximal control of the self by others. It is a later evolutionary development like the neocortex. (Remember, these are metaphors.)

Have you ever felt that at times you were possessed by the devil? Your dreams, thoughts, or actions seem to have come from somewhere else because of their power and your lack of control. At other times you were the opposite, acting almost god-like, which may have been equally puzzling and disturbing. The first feeling may have been emanating principally from a combination of your reptilian and mammalian brains whereas the second stemmed form your cortex and mammalian brain. What was and is happening is that all the parts of your triune brain are always fully functioning. You consciously select which you will focus upon, except those times the force of one or a combination of them literally overpowers you. They all act simultaneously.

While it is true that your brain and your senses are constantly selecting and filtering, your imprinting, conditioning and your conscious choices determine what you will attend to every moment. Right now you are choosing to focus upon this book, but your body is regulating your heart beat and respiration, monitoring your thirst, hunger, and excretions, and a vast array of other critical life-preserving functions. You are experiencing these other things, but you are not attending to them consciously.

Because of these ongoing, simultaneous body/brain activities, as will as the happenings in your external environment, you are bombarded with stimuli. Therefore, inner conflict is unavoidable because each system, organ, even each cell has its own agenda and purposes. The feeling that you are being torn apart is not neurotic, imaginary, symbolic, or metaphorical, but is based on physiological fact. You are being torn apart, every waking moment.

However, the more you understand how the various parts of your brain act independently as well as in concert with other parts, the easier it will be for you to recognize what your feeling/thinking state is and where it's coming from. It will be easier for you to maintain some semblance of sanity and order despite these inevitable conflicts.

Your reptilian and mammalian portions are necessary for you to recognize and feel what your body needs for basic survival. Often these needs conflict with those imprinted upon you by your family and society, needs which are equally powerful. These conflicts prove that psycho-social forces are as powerful as physiological ones. You are caught in conflict between your needs for dependence, independence, and interdependence, all of which are affected by complex biological processes.

You are at a dinner party. Your glucose level is low and your blood screams at your hypothalamus, "feed me!" Your cortex says that dinner will not be for half an hour. If you are sufficiently in control, your cortex will not allow you to run out for a Big Mac, but will have you wait in accordance with the required social amenities.

You are an individual with personal needs and a social being who must compromise with other individuals. Part of your brain finds this ridiculous; ergo, you are in conflict. Frequently, you must defer one need while another is being met. The more conscious these trade-offs are, the easier they are to cope with.

The triune brain is a physiological reality. There is nothing you can do to change the often conflicting demands of each part. There is no way you can ever meet all these demands at the same time because each wants its demands met right now. At times you can integrate their functions, but most of the time you cannot. You can only make a temporary and uneasy peace with them. The more you learn to recognize and feel how each operates on you (by being honest with your feelings and open with your thoughts), how each interacts with each other and your environment, the less you will feel like the devil is in control.

Unpleasant or unthinkable thoughts to people who believe they are (or should be) good are terrifying because they feel responsible for these thoughts (even evil). Of course, you are somewhat responsible, but these so-called evil thoughts are biologically based selfish needs that will not go away and are quite normal. What is abnormal and damaging is denying that they exist. You can repress them of course, but the demands, the energies will continue to goad or disturb you. And they sneak or burst into bloom in ways that frighten and puzzle you.

These constant terrible internal struggles are biochemical. You are not the battleground between the Devil and God, but between your selfish, individual needs and your selfish social ones. It doesn't make it any less of a struggle, but when you know what you're up against, you can make better choices and learn by reading or listening to your body. Learn from your mistakes. By admitting the existence of these often conflicting biological selves you will be better able to cope with their powers as they fight for your attention and their own immediate (but temporary) supremacy.

Know thy biological and social selves and thou wilt be free(er).

Nineteen

Built-In Errors: Structural Limitations

You'll like this chapter: it's short.

Norbert Weiner states that every animal and machine is limited by its structure. Structures may be extended or modified, but new or different limitations will surface. (I seem to be raining on your parade by adding to your already heavy burdens, but if you grasp the importance of this idea, you will find it easier to live with your limitations.)

Man has developed methods and machines which extend his bodily strengths (hammer, giant crane), enable him to fly (balloons, jets), remain under water (submarine, oxygen tanks), see into physical structures (x-ray, CAT scans), extend his vision (telescope, microscope), and amplify his hearing and speaking (telescope, megaphone). He has created many more things which have greatly extended and enlarged his physical and mental dimensions and abilities, yet each new technology has its finite boundaries, new limits.

Man's cultures, which he has created to overcome certain limits as he has with his other inventions, have extended his powers and abilities, but have placed other kinds of limits upon him. Example: Factories and job specialization have created a surplus of material goods and eased much of man's exhausting labor and freed him to have more leisure time. However, mass production has limited his sense of pride in his work, has isolated him from his feeling of belonging to the earth, and caused more social alienation.

What you are imprinted with limits you. Public education should have freed your mind by teaching you the basic skills of a high tech society. The rigid organizational structures in schools have severely and ineptly imprinted you and have limited your creative abilities. Hundreds of students and teachers were asked what they would do to improve the schools. Almost all parroted minor cosmetic changes, because they were limited by what they'd been taught that school was.

A human being begins his life with the genetic givens which determine his sex, appearance, intelligence, his strengths and weaknesses. He has almost infinite possible combinations, but these do not include becoming a table, orchid, or a lion. His structural realm is restricted to the limitations that make him human.

If you can conceive of life as a wondrous mystery and the solving of endless problems as its goal, you won't become so discouraged when, after resolving one problem, another springs from or surfaces from it. If you recognize that a problem solved carries the seeds from which others will come and accept the challenge to test your mettle and character, you will be operating from your giant self.

Twenty

Delusions of Personal Freedom

Students say, "You can't make me do that! I can do whatever I want." Employees refuse to do even the reasonable things their employers request which are considered part of the responsibilities of their jobs. In their demands to be treated justly, Americans have emphasized their rights to personal freedom and neglected their responsibilities to fulfill their obligations.

Historically man has looked to a god, some sort of supreme being, or even a powerful human leader, and admitted that his freedoms were limited by these authorities. He looked to his parents, elders, or those with skills or abilities he valued and then he accepted the limits these people placed on his freedoms. He recognized and accepted his assigned place in life. His personal worth was dependent on fulfilling criteria created by others whom he saw as more powerful. His freedom of choice ranging from where he could live, the job he would do, even the foods and clothes he wore as well as how he perceived the world was totally determined by others (many of whom were dead for years, centuries, or millenniums).

The entire concept of a self which is separate from a mother, father, family, village, or ethnic identity is probably only a few thousand years old, an evolutionary breakthrough. This concept of a separate self grows in meaning as the individual takes increasing responsibility for his actions. Eden stops being a metaphor and becomes the reality of man trying to use his freedom to control his life productively. When this occurs everything that interferes with freedom is taken as an infringement which must be attacked.

Americans have expended more types of real freedom to a greater percentage of their population than any other people on earth. Although our Founding Fathers wrote the exciting documents which have led to this freedom, they did not have any idea how the Constitution and Bill of Rights would finally affect the concept of individual freedom. These early Americans were from countries which had become colonial powers and severely limited others' freedoms. Our original leaders didn't consider freedom appropriate for children, the poor (most states had some sort of tax which prevented the poor from a voice), most non-white minorities, and women.

As public and private schools increased literacy and America became a major world power we extended individual freedoms and the percentage of those who shared in them. Despite our imperfections we are the freest large nation in human history.

One of the inherent limitations of freedom is that the desire for it appears to be insatiable. The more you have the more you want and believe you deserve.

If, as some of the Founding Fathers realized, each generation knew it had to renew its freedoms through responsibility to the nation as well as itself, there would not be the serious problems which exist. Now, because our freedoms have increased in number and degree and include many groups who were formerly excluded, we are gluttonous. Unlike a gourmet who savors and appreciates what he has, many are making garbage and expecting others to clean up the messes their selfishness creates -- while they violently claim their right to do so.

First let's face some reality. As happened to innocent victims in the past, like the Blacks in America, the Jews in Europe, many of the poor in Southeast Asia and Central America, Americans who enjoy some or a great deal of freedom, can have it removed quickly, permanently. The amount of personal freedom you now have is in some proportion related to the amount of money you have (its liquidity and permanence), your intelligence and knowledge, education, character and personality, courage, creativity, family background (ethnicity), and luck. No matter how much freedom you presently enjoy, you may lose it if you do or are caught doing something which your culture or subculture disapproves of. You can be punished and deprived of freedom by guilt, isolation, ostracism or through the legal system.

Second, your freedoms are seriously limited by your genetic givens. There are some things which you would like to do or want to do better, but you do not have the physical, mental, emotional, skills or the inherent abilities to do so. No matter how much you were to train or learn almost none of you could ever become a world class decathlon champion. Very few could win the Noble Prize because you do not have the right gene structures to enable you to be that extraordinary.

Third, your freedoms are limited even more by the structures in your culture. A slave couldn't become a U. S. President. An Untouchable in India could not be anything higher than his parents were. Until recently a woman could not be a rabbi in any Jewish community even though this was considered one of the highest callings and was of the greatest status.

Fourth, unless you want and are able to survive in some uninhabited area of the world, you can never be completely free because you need other people. The children, adults, and minors, who whine about how they are deprived of their freedoms by others are frequently the same people unwilling to do their share in the boring, daily tasks of running the world. The fact remains that as long as you are dependent (like a child) or interdependent (like a healthy adult) your freedoms will always have many limits.

Freedom is not an absolute but is relative. Absolute freedom is impossible because no human being is intelligent, good, strong, or in any way powerful enough to control all facets of his and others' lives. Tyrants have proven how much freedom can be taken away, but no human has ever had absolute freedom. It is impossible because people's real and legitimate needs, as well as their desired ones, are always in conflict with the needs of others. This state of affairs is inevitable what with limited resources, limited time and space, and human mortality.

Relative freedom can be gained through hard work, responsibility, compromise, trade-offs, and by increasing your awareness of other people's realities and needs. The more you understand how and by whom or what you are being controlled, the greater your number of choices, ergo, greater freedom.

Despite my education and experience I cannot move to the San Diego area. I could get a job there, but I would have to take a twenty thousand dollar a year pay cut. School districts have agreed on a system to keep each from pirating the other's best teachers. The way the salary scale is structured, any teacher with a family and no other income is financially pressured to remain where he is. Of course, I do have a choice. But, since I had seven children to consider, was it a feasible one? I think my freedom has been seriously limited.

We have many freedoms. We have a wider variety of choices in where we want to live, what we eat, clothing, schooling, religion, life style, health care, and entertainment than any people in history. As technology improves our choices multiply. No large nation has ever so greatly expanded the individual freedoms which we enjoy. Yet these are still relative or limited freedoms.

In school I tell the children that they have limited freedoms, but many rights protected by law and customs. I let them know their rights because they deserve to know them. They must earn their freedoms.

They get them by responsible behavior and lose them (briefly) when they are irresponsible -- that is, don't consider the freedoms of others. If I break or violate natural or man-made laws, get caught, and am convicted, I pay a price. My freedoms are limited first because I know the possible consequences of breaking a law and second if I am punished by others. This is merely an awareness of logical and reasonable consequences within a society.

Personal freedom is a delusion if you think it means you are able to do whatever you want. It is a delusion if you think you are not affected by what others think and do. It is a delusion if you think what you do doesn't have any effect upon others. You can escape many of the limits placed upon your freedoms by realistically appraising your abilities (which include your courage, energy, and will), learning what is necessary to be interdependent, and becoming flexible in your thinking and behavior. Strangely enough, the more unselfish you are the more freedoms you seem to have.

By admitting your freedoms are relative and limited, preparing yourself with many alternatives, you are acting from your giant self and are realistically expanding your freedoms.

Twenty-One

Improvement, Not Perfectiom

The chapter heading was originally a typo, but I realized it helped dramatize my point. As you go about the daily business of your life and attempt to create and express your giant self you will be making mistakes constantly. It is not only human to err, but errors are opportunities for growth, for the creation of your giant self.

I think one of the main problems with self-help books is that the writer and reader enter into an unhealthy collusion. The writer promises much more than he can deliver because he wants to please the reader -- and sell copies and make the big bucks. The reader wants the easiest path, the quick fix.

I would like to be rich and famous and be the latest guru on talk radio and TV too. However, at fifty-eight, I'd rather make a lasting impression on a few than make a brief imprint on many. I believe that the ideas I've shared already and the ones to come can greatly improve your life. As much as I hate cutesy, catchy phrases, I must admit that they are effective as learning aids. As a teacher I use them because anything that makes learning more effective I use (if the learning is valuable).

Therefore, if you keep in mind that you are expressing your giant self when you admit you are an imperfect being and then seek constant improvement, not perfection, you will grow slowly, but your growth will be substantial.

It's like those who try to lose weight rapidly. They are doomed to failure in almost direct proportion to the speed and amount they lose. Those who lose weight rapidly tend to confuse their metabolic processes. What happens is that when less food is eaten it is transformed into fat more easily and quickly. The quick fix has a rebound effect and most gain more weight in an endless cycle of dieting and weight loss, followed by greater weight gain. Those who lose slowly tend to gradually change their life styles and eating habits and it's the change in their lives that makes a permanent difference in their weight.

The same with these ideas. If every time you felt flushed, embarrassed, confused, and physiologically ill you reminded yourself that you're probably operating from your diminished self, you will bring this awareness into your consciousness. Once the process becomes second nature, you can then consciously determine who and what is (or has been) causing your diminished self to surface. Each time, after you have dealt with it, you will know that you are acting from your giant self.

If you have the modest goal of improvement, not perfection, then your giant self will grow in steady increments and you will find yourself operating from it more often. There is no way you can live in society in which others evaluate and judge you so that you can ever totally escape your diminished self.

Admitting, facing, and using that will insure the steady growth of your giant self.

Part Two

Battlegrounds Of The
Giant Versus Diminished Selves

Twenty-Two

Fears

Fear is often the common denominator between the expression of the giant or diminished self. Many fears are unavoidable and are useful for safety or self-preservation. In these instances fear is intelligent, therefore comes form the giant self. Sometimes, in those moments when you are in real danger, feel fear, but perform an act in an effort to save another human, this capacity emanates from the giant self. In fact, these instances often are peak experiences, when you transcend your fears of a real danger to help another, you feel such "at-oneness with the other person, yourself, and a spirituality" that you are permanently transformed. (Of course, if you die in the process, you are permanently transformed, but unable to share the experience.)

Experiencing fear of events, beliefs, or people who pose a danger to life, limb, or dignity can all be expressions of the giant self if you have emotional and intellectual awareness of the dangers and the courage to face them.

If you perform an apparently courageous act, but do not feel fear, the act is not heroic. Such an act is from the diminished self and neither ennobles nor teaches you anything. A hero (giant self) has a deep passion and love of life, but knowingly risks death or danger because he intuitively or intellectually feels a cosmic bond with every person and object.

Most fears are not cosmic, heroic, or based on real danger to the person. Most fears are irrational. They are taught by society in every culture's efforts to tame the powerful and selfish forces of self-preservation that drive each human. These fears are real and many believe are necessary if a culture is to survive. I believe that this necessity was true, but is not so now. Man has the capabilities of controlling his built-in, biologically selfish impulses and motives when he understands, feels, and is taught his connections with everything in the universe. Once he realizes that Donne's statement, "No man is an island!" is not a metaphor but reality, then he can willingly make the compromises, the adjustments to help himself and his world without coercion.

No boss needs to force me to go to work and do the best job I can. I do my best because I have a deep concern for my students and their place in the world. I operate from my giant self. If a supervisor begins to impose his beliefs on me, no matter how overtly or subtly, he is operating from his fears, his diminished self, and places me in a position in which it is difficult for me not to respond from my own diminished self. This does not mean I cannot learn from him. I can take suggestions from him when they come from his greater knowledge, some of which is due to his position and access to information I do not possess. If I did not listen to him, then I would be responding from my fears, my diminished self. My fears would place limits upon me.

Finally, there are many fears with little foundation in reality. These all come from the diminished self, but usually have been imposed upon you by others and by the culture. Some fears are the result of your misinterpretation of reality or of dangers. All these fears, no matter where they come from are real to you! Your ability to cope with and use them for your benefit is determined by how strongly they have been imprinted upon you, how aware you are of how and by whom they were created, the degree of actual danger they reflect, and your courage and will in facing the possible consequences of confronting your fears.

Let us consider Realistic Fears:

You will die! Death is definitely in your future. You do not want to die. At birth there were some genetic givens which determine when you will die. However, these are not absolutes so by learning your body and how to best care for it, you can extend your life beyond its genetically given time.

You have no control over the fact that you will die, but you have some control about when. Since death is a realistic fear, it is healthy to admit and face it. The fear can mobilize you to absorb information and learn the behaviors that will delay death's inevitability. The sense of control, though limited, helps you develop a value system to stop an unnecessary preoccupation with death. Thus, you can spend more of your life living through your giant self.

Most people fear aging. Aging brings you closer to death, but it also heralds the weakening of your powers, chronic pain, and increasing dependency. Further, whereas in other times older people were venerated for their wisdom, in our society old age equals uselessness. It is the culture of the young. Young minds have less imprints, less programming, and are more flexible to meet the technological and biological changes that are occurring at such a rapid rate. With aging the ability to rapidly memorize and retain new information and the physiological rate of responses are slower. On the other hand older minds have more memories to access and, if stimulated, can build larger and stronger structures than young ones.

Technological breakthroughs, now mostly team efforts, usually come from minds which have absorbed the previous information in the discipline or field, but are young enough, flexible enough to challenge the accepted dogma. Even the wisdom which comes from the experiences of living can now be transferred, absorbed, and utilized by a managerial class which is younger and younger. (Actually, age is not as important as knowledge and the ability to see the data in a fresh perspective.)

Aging in the past was a badge of honor, but it is now a realistic fear. You will not be venerated, you will be considered a social burden. You are a burden to yourself, your family, your society. Your ego is smashed as you learn to be increasingly useless and dependent. You have all the liabilities of a child, but none of his cuteness and promise. You are without a future! (This is not true and does not happen to people who continue to operate from their giant selves.)

This is worse and occurs earlier with most women. Women are the caretakers, the nurturers, the first teachers. They are also discarded first. Those who have elected to serve their families unselfishly find their former behaviors are burdens upon their loved ones. The behaviors which were helpful are now constricting the growth of others. They are obsolete. Many actually die while others die inside and take to drink, drugs, or meaningless activities to fill time. This defeatism is unnecessary.

Research indicates that like the fear of death, the fear of aging can be confronted and used by the giant self to make your life better. It takes a change of attitude. You need to understand that those who live the most useful, productive, and happy lives do so until the moment of their death. Joseph Campbell was a vibrant man until he died at eighty-three. I heard Roger Williams speak when he was the same age and he was funny and articulate. (I could have beat him in the 100 yard dash. So what?)

To forestall the moment of your death and not be defeated by aging you need to function within your giant self. This means having a comfortable sense of your self in the big picture of the cosmos. It means attending to the research that says those people who care for others and share the intimacies of their lives with others live longer and more happily. It means constantly using your mind and body and gently pushing their limits. It means expressing your creative and spiritual selves regardless of age.

Most humans fear death and aging because both seem to imply the extinction of the self, the ego. Those who do not seem to fear death and aging are those who have a strong belief in some sort of continuation of the self in some other place or time. Some have less fear because they feel the self will be continued through family or culture and they do not feel a separation between these entities and themselves. These would be true ecologists.

Some of the delusions about human dignity can limit your options, I personally do not relish the thought of being led about, pushed in a wheelchair, or confined to bed in which a stranger feeds, washes, and wipes me. If I get to a vegetative, non human stage, I have requested that my life be terminated because I believe that merely being alive does not mean I am human. I correlate being human with consciousness, awareness, and control.

Now consider Unrealistic Fears.:

These are fears that are the result of some person or institution unconsciously or consciously making you fearful in some way to control your behavior. I will discuss these fears at some length, because they are the ones that are the substance of your diminished self. Once you understand how they have been created you will be prepared to confront and deal with them.

There are also the fears that spring from your personal experiences and somehow you either misinterpreted or overreacted to their alleged dangers. These are fears that are not shared by the general public, but may be shared by a large number of people. These may be fears that have some basis in reality, but your reaction is unrealistic. Black widow spiders can bite. Their bite can cause discomfort, illness, and in a very few cases (usually children who are not treated) death. A healthy respect for black widow spiders is therefore normal. However, if you won't go into the garage, the backyard, or your fear makes you incapable of reasonable thought and action, then it's unrealistic and is a reflection of your diminished self.

In the next few chapters I will examine how our social institutions train you to be fearful as a means to control you. They induce fears which play to and create your diminished self. They make you less human. You don't have to be vulnerable. You can learn instead to function and express your giant self.

Twenty-Three

Diminished Self: Prenatal, Childhood

I was taught that animals could not think, that almost all of their behaviors were instinctual, mechanical. Since then the number of things animals do that are now identified as thinking has increased exponentially in the higher species and some form of thought has been found to exist in animals as low on the evolutionary scale as one-celled organisms. A fascinating find is that sometimes when one member of a species or variety learns a useful new way of solving a problem he not only can teach it to others like himself, but somehow his and their DNA/RNA cell structures change so that the learning becomes a behavior which is passed on to the next generation -- without the need for it to be taught.

I was taught that babies (in utero and for a few months afterwards) are blobs of growing protoplasm. For many months after birth they could only see movement, hear chaotic noises, and that even touch was not a developed sense.

Now there is increasing evidence that a baby is an informational sponge with its senses and brain quite highly developed. In fact, the young are being stimulated and developed while they are in utero. Embryos and babies, like animals, probably learn much more than we realize. Obviously their levels of thought don't approximate what we consider quality thinking, but then some adults would be disqualified if the definition of thought was too exacting.

Even before the child is conceived the amount and kinds of drugs, tobacco, sugars, and caffeine the parents ingest affect the genetic structures of their eggs and sperm. So, it isn't just the parents' past genetic structures which affect their potential offspring, but what they do to their bodies up to several months before the child is conceived.

At the moment of conception the history of both parents and all their ancestors are potential helpers or hindrances to the child. The health of both parents is a critical contribution to a healthy child.

Although it is an old wives' tale that if you think certain thoughts while pregnant they will result in problems for the child, it is true that the parents' mental/emotional health as well as their physical health will affect the child. It makes good sense that a mother who is disturbed or malnourished is not going to have as healthy a child as she would have had if she had been healthier. Yet, everyone can point to children born from the most disturbed, unhealthy parents who have entered the world in amazingly robust good health and continued to have it despite horrendous environmental conditions. What they don't consider is what those children might have been under favorable conditions.

After all, the growing embryo shares the nutrients, the poisons, all the pluses and minuses of health the mother brings to her body. Her thoughts don't just happen in some small portion of her brain, but are an orchestration of every cell and organ system of her body. Her thoughts are experienced biochemically and biologically within her body. If stress and disease of the mind can cause physical problems for the mother, they must affect the embryo the same ways. This does not mean that if she fears or thinks of monsters her child will be born like a monster. It means if she is stressed she will not process her nutrients as well, her body will not function as well, and the child may be deprived of small amounts of things he needs for optimum growth. The result could range from minor food sensitivities to serious malformations or malfunctioning organs.

These stresses could also result in the child having learned fears in utero which cannot be traced on any other way. Suppose the mother has a fear of heights and every time she crosses a bridge, climbs a ladder, or peers over a ledge her body chemistry reflects these fears. This chemical bath passes into her blood stream. This is shared by the embryo. The messages (and fears) become permanently stored in the mother -- why not in the embryo?

If the embryo is not a blob, but a feeling and thinking (to varying degrees) entity like his mother, then he should be experiencing feelings and thoughts simultaneously with her. Of course, he does not share her previous experience which brought on these feelings nor does he have her fully developed feeling and thinking systems. Therefore he cannot derive the same meanings from the chemical bath and experiences. He may only have diffuse and nonspecific anxiety when certain chemicals or situations cause his brain to fire part of these messages.

Whereas the mother's experience of the fears and stresses have some historical precedents residing in her memories which allow her to make sense of, to give a perspective to the experience, the embryo has none. He cannot connect the fears with any reasonable, logical experience because he is too underdeveloped to do so. This creates the worst possible fears, those that are diffuse, unlocalized, and therefore difficult to change or cure. Your groundless fears may well belong to your mother (or father). Isn't it marvelous to logically blame someone else?

Of course, some fears may be genetic. As mentioned with animals some learnings appear to become part of a species' genetic givens. The same would apply to humans. These genetic givens may have been transmitted through many generations and have significant survival value. Remember, fears, like pain, are often extremely useful for the protection and survival of the organism or species.

There are other modes of communication between the fetus and the mother. When you love, you sense the other when she's in danger. Even her happiness, sadness, dreams, and thoughts may be felt by you when you're apart. You can sense it during love-making, quietly together, or even across great time spans and distances. Scientists have not proven the exact nature of this energy, phenomenon, or method of communication, but the holographic paradigm by Karl Pribram and David Bohm gives one possible explanation.

A hologram is a picture taken by a combination of direct and refracted light. The picture it makes is totally unrecognizable until you shine a special light through it and it takes on a three-dimensional effect. In a hologram all things are interrelated and interconnected. Tearing even a tiny fragment from anywhere in the picture and then shining a light into it gives you the entire picture. The larger the piece the cleared the reproduction.

The fetus and the other, you and your lover, are totally interconnected. The more you share (the more information, the more powerful hologram), the less of the hologram needs to be stimulated in order for you to get a message. It's as if you're in a small, still pool. If your lover makes the slightest movement you immediately sense it. Much of what is called extrasensory perception (ESP) is a perturbation of the hologram you share with everyone and everything in the universe, but ESP is especially sensitive to certain key people in your life.

You, your loved one (fetus or adult), each of you apparently separated are, in reality ... one. I am trying to get you to listen to the messages of your mind/body so that you can more accurately read them. The same process applies in intimate relationships. When you begin to feel as if you are one, then whatever happens within each will be sensed and felt by the other. This is only a rare occurrence because the experience can be frightening and disconcerting. In these days of weak emotional commitment to any other person, being in a holographic framework with another person is seen as taking away something from one's individuality. And an emotional commitment is frightening because you first have to give more than you receive. This is irrational to competitive people.

How do you learn this feeling of oneness with another? You knew how when you were a fetus and after you were born, but the more socialized and cerebral you became, the more you lost it. Love, when it is full and passionate enough to block thought and socialization, forces you and your lover into an ongoing hologram and your sensitivities are recaptured. They are lost again when the stresses and pressures of daily life create two separate entities from the crucible of oneness.

As a fetus you and your mother were a hologram. Whatever she experienced, you shared and vice-versa. Mothers have reported feelings of dread, of something bad happening to the fetus, which were confirmed. Of course this phenomenon could be said to be chemical rather than holographic, but why are the explanations necessarily mutually exclusive? Both may be correct. Nature has provided all living things with complex back-up systems. In these cases fear was a useful warning mechanism whether it was chemical or holographic or both.

Therefore, your mother's fears, joys, emotions, and thoughts were communicated to you genetically, chemically, electrically, holograph-ically, and in other ways not yet described nor understood.

Although not as intimate physically as you and your mother, your father or other family members could also play critical roles in imprinting you -- in good and bad ways. Suppose your father is having serious financial troubles. Being thoughtful he doesn't mention it, but his general anxiety pervades the home and permeates into all the relations. Your mother and you, part of a hologram which includes all three of you, pick up and are affected by his anxiety.

As a therapist I have dealt with people who can't find the causes of their fears. Sometimes this is due to my ineptitude or their inabilities to be honest, but I now believe that some of their fears were not theirs, but came from their parents and were imprinted upon them. This is why it is so important to understand, admit, and take responsibility for your fears. This is the only way you can ever find out whether they belong to you or were imposed upon you by others.

There are several theories that emphasize the damage that occurs during birth. They fall into two main classes, those that believe the process itself is painful and these memories are permanently etched into the child's brain and the other which believes that it is the separation from mother that results in a lifetime of fear and insecurity and a desire to return to the nurturing womb.

The holographic concept would lend credibility to these theories. However, most fears could also be explained as the result of the child's history after leaving the womb. Life is fraught with frustration and dangers and even the most independent person has strong dependency needs which he may mask or deny, but which exist within him. No one would deny that birth must be painful and frightening to the emerging child. However, nature has a solution.

It is believed that many animals when they are caught by predators and are being eaten alive, enter a state of grace. These animals do not feel pain nor are they afraid because their bodies produce morphine-like chemicals that anesthetize them. The same happens to humans at death, at times of great stress, and I believe that this occurs with the baby during birth. If this is true then he does not suffer his birth traumas, but still might share his mother's.

Therefore, I think the mother should be helped to have as painless a delivery as possible. The father, mother, and other family members should be allowed to participate in a birth hologram, each making the experience as pleasant as possible, sharing the pain, but making whatever pain occurs take place in an environment filled with a sense of communion. Thus, the process of birth becomes equally as important as is the moment of birth.

Another way of looking at it is to accept the pain as a way of teaching the baby about its inevitability. No human can live a full life without much pain. It is a message -- pain can be useful in indicating the need for change. Personally, I would favor the least painful birth.

From the moment of birth you are socialized to fit the needs of your family and society. Your needs are net within a context that is best for others who are more powerful. Much of what is done to you is not done maliciously or consciously to hurt you, but just turns out badly. They know not what they do...

Feeding: You are dependent on your mother for your very existence. (Many children are raised by mother surrogates, but I will refer only to Mother.) You are totally helpless for many years. You quickly learned which behaviors got you food and which didn't. Although you had your own internal time schedules for feeding, you had to gradually adjust your feedings to fit the family's organization. This meant that you had to learn to ignore your body's biochemical messages and follow an imposed schedule. These messages of genetic bodily rhythms are altered by amount of activity, sleep, weather, anxiety, and a host of other variables, but you had to learn to ignore them. It was the beginning of an alienation from your body. After all, if you cannot have your needs met, you have to tell your body not to react to normal internal stimuli and to obey the externally imposed ones. Most people make this adjustment, this trade-off of family convenience, but it is part of much of your illnesses and your alienation from your body.

Urination and defecation: Your bodily wastes were not a big problem to you. They just happened to you and were expressed with the same lack of concern pigeons display. Without a diaper you would have continued to be responsive to your eliminative rhythms and would have left your presents everywhere.

When man was nomadic this may have been acceptable even for adults, but as soon as he began staying in one place, waste disposal became a health problem. In a modern society it is very serious because your presents, even in a diaper, makes others aware of your presence. This is embarrassing to your mother so she is pressured to make you control your wastes at specific times. This further alienates you from your body because here again you are not allowed to follow your bodily rhythms, but must conform to a rhythm imposed upon you.

Physiologically this control gets to be more serious as you get older and results in hemorrhoids, stomach, intestinal, bladder and kidney disorders, even some forms of cancer. Psychologically it makes you believe your body is smelly, dirty, and disgusting because these unpleasant things come out of it. You are taught to believe this so you will control these responses and force your body to follow rhythms which are not natural to you, but fit family and society's wishes.

I am not suggesting that your mother should have let you make your deposits anywhere you wished without regard for other people. However, when she responded with an academy award performance of gagging, screaming, or hitting you while telling you how stinky you were, this was not taken lightly by you. Some people cannot get enough deodorant or soap to eliminate their feeling that they stink! To stink is to be unwelcome, despised, and unloved -- even unlovable. (I knew two sisters who shaved their bodies completely and took enemas and douches daily in an obsessive effort to feel clean -- and lovable. It didn't help; they always felt filthy.)

These things that are excreted by your body come from and are part of you. Although your mother wanted you to know you were accepted and loved, but not your excretions, you felt that she was rejecting you -- unless you kept them secret and away from her. You could not separate yourself from her loathing towards your waste products and you felt she loathed you. (Maybe she did, maybe you were loathable.) So, you learned to hate these evil-smelling products of your body and generalized to self-hate or maybe you hated your rectum, anus, and genitals. Actually, many raw and cooked foods smell worse than normal excretions. It is not just their odors, but the value judgements we make about them that cause them to be so unpleasant to us.

You bought these value judgements and so you are distressed or disgusted by these odors in a learned self-loathing which is perpetuated by further social conditioning. To be told that you stink is one of the most insulting things that can be said about you. You also associate this as proof of something inherently (within) unpleasant, bad, or evil about you. And, it never goes away. It perpetuates your diminished self.

Sleep: Besides controlling your food intake and excretion schedules, you were told how many hours a night you must sleep. Now, if you had been told you must stay in your bedroom eight to ten hours so your parents could have some time alone and you could have slept as many or as few hours as you needed then that would have made some sense. But, you were supposed to be in bed, quiet, with your eyes closed, and be sleeping according to whatever schedule your parents believed necessary.

It is known now that individual requirements for sleep vary greatly. A few healthy people have never slept their entire lives. Many people are comfortable with three to four hours whereas some need ten to twelve or more to be friendly and healthy. These individual rhythms are affected by stress, food intake, general health, age, and other factors. Suffice it to say each one of us is different and our health depends upon our abilities to listen and be responsive to our bodily sleep rhythms.

Your parents didn't allow you to find your natural rhythms. They wanted time away from you. They believed that eight or ten hours was a necessity for everyone. They may have imposed their unique sleep patterns upon you because these patterns were healthy for them. As with your eating and excretory rhythms you were forced to ignore your own sleep rhythms for those imposed upon you. Many negative reinforcements can be created by forcing you to stay in bed when you're not tired or sleepy.

Instead of being angry with your parents who probably thought they were acting in your best interests, begin to allow yourself to find the bodily rhythms that best fit you. You can't just listen to your body because it doesn't understand how to get back to its original genetic givens. It will take many months for you to know what are your real rhythms and those which have been imposed upon you and are now habit. You may find this project very difficult because of your present patterns of school, work, or family.

I realized that I may have selected a profession (teaching) which perpetuated a pattern of restricted and scheduled rhythms. I suffered form many embarrassing and painful problems until I refused to be the slave of the system. I now follow my rhythms and I allow my students to do the same. I have been much healthier, happier, and so have my students.

If you decide to follow your own rhythms you may get static from family, friends, and in your work, but by some judicious compromises you can greatly improve your overall health and still live with others, It means eating less or more depending upon how hungry you are and possibly snacking at times which seem odd to those in a different rhythm. It means eliminating when necessary and not during prescribed breaks. It means sleeping, napping, or resting when necessary. Sleep should be a wonderful, refreshing, and happy experience. If it is associated with fear, punishment, and parental anger, it leaves imprints that haunt you all your life.

It is likely that most people with sleeping problems or disorders would not have them if they had been allowed to find their own rhythms and if these had been respected by their parents. (Of course, some sleep disturbances are temporary and caused by illness, work, family stress, or change in routines.)

Of our seven children, the twins were the youngest and the only ones raised by us from birth to adulthood. Marie and I made most of our mistakes with our other children. We were much more tolerant of the twins' eating, sleeping, and bodily rhythms. Consequently, they are healthy, happy, and very sensitive to their unique rhythms. Neither has any problems and eats, sleeps, or eliminates according to his/her needs and the appropriateness of the situation. We did place some demands on them, but they did not experience anywhere near the pressures the other children did.

My suggestions to you are to think through how your parents imprinted you. How did they force their arbitrary rhythms upon you. Examine your life now. How many problems that you have can be traced to these early imprints?

When you do this search for your own rhythms you must realize that you will still have to live in a social setting so you will need to make compromises. If more relaxed scheduled are discussed with those who will be affected and they can be persuaded to have some latitude and understanding, then adjustments will be much easier, more pleasant, and more effective.

Your prenatal, birth, and childhood imprints will never be totally extinguished, but you can modify them through sensitive listening to your body, responding to its messages, and patiently working with those affected by your changes.

Twenty-Four

Religion and Your Diminished Self

Naturally, I think I've got something valuable to share, but you may not agree or be ready for it. Therefore you need to know where I'm coming from. Depending on what I've eaten, whether I'm depressed or happy, and a host of other complex variables, I'm either theist, pantheist, or atheist. Sometimes, I'm even Jewish or Buddhist or Hindu or a Confucian (maybe just confused?).

You could get me to believe in a god. If you held a gun to Marie's head or any of my children and said, "Say you believe in my god!" I would immediately say it. If like many of the Fundamentalists you said, "Pray to God and your prayers will be answered." and I constantly saw that they were, I'd probably believe in God.

However, in one case I was pressured to believe out of fear, in the other because I was greedy and wanted to have everything I wanted (especially the things I didn't deserve or need). In these examples and in the vast majority of those associated with religion, I see the pathetic workings of the diminished self. The diminished self is fearful, selfish, dependent, and parasitic.

I feel that the creators of religions were usually those who were expressing their giant selves. Their idea was to share their spiritual, moral, and ethical visions with others so the common man could each more easily have what the creators suffered to achieve. It's like a loving parent who wants to save his children from going through his pains. Unfortunately, there is no real spirituality without a quest.

This quest may be intellectual (Confucius); aesthetic (Beethoven); experimental/spiritual (Jesus). There are some criteria which make the quest difficult, which is why most people opt for the easy way out through a prescribed ritualistic religion. The quest is a learning experience which, even with the help of a teacher or guru must be faced -- alone. A quest is the ultimate test of man's courage, creativity, and will. It is a transforming experience. A person who was a common man emerges an extraordinary, an uncommon one. He or she has transcended his physiological and psychological limits, which is why so many have so-called extrasensory powers and experiences. The rigors of the quest force them to overcome all the sociological and psychological limitations I have explained as man's common cultural experiences. The questors see clearly the world as it is, but they also realize that perception is man-made and have forged a broader vision for themselves and others. Their mistake is believing that their quests and maps are the only way to achieve the giant self or a transcendent vision. What they can each be is a different model for the common man to emulate and inspire. A successful model is proof that the quest is possible, and worth the enormous effort!

To me religion is the institutionalizing of rituals which are substitutes for each person learning to become spiritually strong. Suppose a scrawny person wanted to be Mr. America, but instead of years of exercise, wise food choices, and healthy living patterns, he wore a fancy jockstrap, went into a room once or twice a week with others like him, and they all prayed for a great body. I know he would fail because the road to a great body takes commitment and years of effort (which is why I don't pose for any muscle magazines or disrobe where there are mirrors).

I sincerely believe the road to a great spirit is infinitely more arduous because it takes even greater commitment and self-discipline as well as years of thought, prayer, and/or meditation, and constant unselfishness. Especially the last is impossible for those trapped in their diminished selves. Religion perpetuates the diminished self.

Religions are like an appendix: they hang around and serve no useful function. Unfortunately, unlike the appendix, they continuously poison the body/mind. And, no surgeon's knife can remove them, so they are allowed to do their damage. Worse, they are believed useful, so they are not taxed nor can anyone argue against them without being seen as evil or demented -- a danger to society. In fact, the religions are the real danger because they prevent their followers from finding real spirituality. They lull their followers away from the arduous road towards spirituality by appealing to their normal human fears, their pettiness, their diminished selves and through rituals and practices that are pallid substitutes for confrontations and intimacies with the divine.

The rise of Satanism and its violence is a regression to primitive practices as well as indicating a serious need to make a total spiritual commitment. In no way am I condoning the practices of Satanic worship. I am saying its revival points to the fact that most Judeo-Christian religions have lost their emotional hold on their members. Most excuse or forgive all misdeeds or misbehaviors of their members. They demand very little emotionally or spiritually. The Catholic Church is an example. In an effort to become modern, which was meant to keep its membership high, it compromised its powerful rituals and narrowly focused laws. Instead of gaining, it has lost the mystic appeal and magic it once had.

I am not a proponent of Catholicism, but it had the virtue of leading many people into a true spiritual quest. I don't think it offers that anymore.

Religions were a useful step in the evolution of man's spiritual quest. I believe they still could serve a purpose for millions of people. If they could be seen as a beginning of spirituality I wouldn't object to them. If they gave people a thoughtful and loving basis in which to deal with others I would be pleased. As it is now, religions tend to encourage their members' fears of others and the expressions of these fears in narrow-mindedness the results of which run the gamut from daily discourteousness and emotional abuse to genocide based on intellectual rationalizations.

Those who wished to be secure and nurtured could remain at a beginning spiritual level all their life. This would be alright as long as they damaged no one else. Those who wished to go to higher, more demanding levels would recognize that their spiritual quest would take them far away from the comforting arms of their religion. They would understand that their quest would mean questioning everyone and everything they believed in and confronting the fears and (alleged) evils within them as well as the devils and dangers outside of themselves. Much of what they endured they could get help with from their professors (gurus), but their level tests, or their graduation would depend on what they faced -- alone.

The payoff would be that they could move freely within their former religions and among their friends and loved ones with greater understanding, appreciation, and love. They would be living within the ever-expanding boundaries of their giant selves. The questors would have such a strong sense of personal identity (which paradoxically can only occur when they have faced the frightening Unknowable alone and have shed their individuality) and such a wider world view that the pettiness and trivialities that plague most humans would not affect them. They would be immersed in real living while taking life's tribulations and trials in stride because of their expanding spirituality and unique perspective.

If you are to truly experience all you can of your giant self you must search out, find, and begin your spiritual quest. I do not think it can be done within any religion -- unless you wish to go no further than beginning spirituality. There is no one specific path, but you must blaze your own. You can be helped by many individuals and institutions in your quest, but your greatest challenges and successes must be experienced --*alone*.

In the name of Gods and religions man has perpetrated every conceivable evil upon other men. I know man is not a rational being. He only uses logic and reason to give substance to the things he does which spring from his emotions. I'm more comfortable with a person who says that he's going to kill me because he wants my wife than one who wants to kill me because I'm godless or won't believe in his conception of God. Religious people make me nervous because they feel they have a mandate from God to do anything their reptilian or limbic brains tell them.

Nowadays, God is love, at least to millions of Christians and Jews. I admit this is an improvement over the fearful Jehovah of the Bible, but I am confused as to how he is supposed to express love to me and I to him. You see, in my definition of love there is reciprocity. I can worship, idolize, or appreciate God, but I cannot love him because I don't have the faintest idea of what I could do that he could possible want or need. Of course there are millions of people willing to tell me exactly what God wants or needs from me. They are the same type who believed the earth was flat and cheered as Bruno and other scientists were burned at the stake.

I am egotistical, but I hope I never tell others what the greatest power in the Universe said just to me. God has been described as omnipotent, omnipresent, omniscient, ineffable, and unknowable. I guess that pretty much covers it all. God is everywhere at the same time, doing everything, and is all powerful, but we cannot know him because he is invisible and his actions are beyond our human abilities to understand. That's about as intimidating as any cluster of statements could be.

Religion is useful. It has helped men intimidate others to do their bidding. It plays to the diminished self which wants simple explanations and certainty. Religion has done and does that. How else could one group of men get loving parents to give up their teen age children to sacrifice them to a god so he would give them good fortune? How could religious leaders allow their congregations to participate in atrocities or turn their backs on them even when committed against their own countrymen? I'm not speaking just of Europeans, but Americans too. We have participated in the genocide of Native Americans, murder in every minority group, and still are quiet while millions of our lower class (because of economic conditions which most of the rest of us profit from) live within or on the fringes of desperate, soul-killing poverty.

So-called primitive religions and our modern ones are the result of man's fragility in the face of fearsome natural forces over which he has very limited control. Religions give us explanations which work as pacifiers to our fears. Science replaced religion for many of us, but at some point it resulted in the same problems. Both science and religion can be used to explain phenomena (with science ahead) but both also are abused in the ways they are used to control people.

I would not mind if religions retained all the music, art, dance, and rituals that are entertaining and ennobling. I am not against making people feel good. I am against them feeling good at someone else's expense. I am in favor of people searching within themselves and if the company of others helps, then well and good.

What I have seen and experienced is the naked fear of religious people when others challenge their shaky beliefs. I say shaky because if they were strong they wouldn't have to proselyte (as I'm doing, but I admit I'm scared and vulnerable) and try to convince others.

The more who believe a thing the more certain one can be of its truth.

That last statement is untrue.

All new ideas came from the minds of a few who went against the vast majority. As soon as a new truth becomes common knowledge, someone else is on the verge of yet another insight.

I will be more generous than my detractors. Just as there are levels of physical, mental, and emotional development and each person has a wide range of genetic givens, there are levels of spiritual development. There are those who must believe in religions as practiced in the Stone Age. Some have a powerful pantheism which sees gods everywhere. Some need the beauty and security of a religion which is highly ritualized. Others see religion as a social, ethnic, or cultural expression of many complex needs. Some see it as a wholesome mode to explore higher levels of ethics and morality. Each view can be useful and an expression of some person's path to his giant self.

However, if a religion mainly controls its adherents and they remain in a static, dependent stage, then it is unhealthy and damaging. If it makes them narrow-minded and petty and they need to feel superior at the expense of others then that religion is dangerous.

For most people the bad outweighs the good as far as what their religion does for them. In this negative category I place all those religious believers presently engaged in holy wars all over the world. They are caught in a time warp. These people are moving from tribalism to nationalism in a world which has shrunk into ever increasing interdependency. Religions (as they were) and nationalism (as it is) controls people's minds and emotions in ways that prevent them from creating their giant selves.

I wish this were not true because both religion and nationalism gave such certainty to people's lives. Certainty and creating a giant self are contradictions!!

You may not agree with me but that's alright because people who totally agree with me bore me. After all what can we talk about? If everything that's brought up causes us to nod our heads in agreement, how can we learn, how can we grow? I love to argue, not because I want to win or prove how smart I am (although if that happens I may appear smug), but that's how I learn. I really do listen to the other person. I want to understand his genetics, his experiences, and how he managed to come to such an absurd conclusion when the truth is so obvious to me. I love to argue about religion with a person who has conviction, who wants to convert (teach) me, but who does so from his giant self. This person doesn't need to insult or degrade me, but speaks to me as if I had a brain, heart and soul. (I do have these things, but often I am spoken to as if my parents couldn't afford them all for me.) If my arguments are intelligent, I have no heart or soul. If they are filled with love and compassion then I am without a brain.

Religious discussions inevitably deal with everything that's important in life, as well as facing the meaning of life which includes death and whatever comes after. All religions attempt to understand a god or gods or a powerful universal force. However, all define a god as unknowable, but then, without batting an eye, explain who and what he is.

Religious professionals, like any other professionals, are taught and believe in a specific system. Why they accept one system over another depends on their individual histories, not on some absolute truth, which, if it existed would eventuate in one world religion.

Therefore there seem to be many viable and reliable roads to deal with that which is unknowable, all powerful, and ever present. My viewpoint is that if we each speak to one another from our giant selves, not our fragile, diminished selves, we would not have to agree with one another, but we could respect each other and realize that our differences are not to be feared, but are God's way of teaching us about His incredible powers and diversity. As we learn, are more loving and compassionate, we (as expressions of our giant selves) increase the dimensions of God.

Of course, this is just one way of approaching a god and religion, but it is a peaceful, thoughtful, and loving way. It is one which will increase your giant self.

Twenty-Five

Work and Your Diminished Self

Most people spend more than half of their waking hours going to, coming from, or at work. For most of them their job is just that – a job. It is something that must be done because it pays for the things that they need or want, the things that make life possible and meaningful.

The separation between the classes is pronounced at work. The blue collar workers mostly come from the lower and lower middle classes. The people who work at desks come from the same and the middle classes. Their bosses come from the middle and upper middle classes. (The upper class, the old, inherited, and new rich who control the majority of the world's capital, have little contact with and are generally unknown to the other classes.) The same prejudices and misconceptions about each other that existed as an undercurrent in public schools are more obvious in the workplace and the consequences of not honoring these differences are much more serious.

Movies try to glamorize the myth of the lower class girl or boy who meets and marries someone higher up on the social ladder and lives happily ever after. This does occur occasionally and gives some validity to the myth, but most people do not move beyond their birth class. Attitudes of superiority-inferiority are strong at work. There is an unstated assumption of some intrinsic superiority in each person above you in the organizational hierarchy. This inequality shows in many ways.

When a subordinate is in the presence of his boss there is deference in physical space. The boss can move into the other's space, but the subordinate cannot. Any touching or intimacy is strictly controlled by the boss. The boss signals when the sub may speak, how long, and with how much intensity. Eye contact reminds one of wolves and other animals with a prescribed power hierarchy. Americans love to talk about their freedom and how democratic their institutions are, but it's more smoke than fire.

There are specified rules of conduct if a sub wishes to speak to those higher on the hierarchy than his immediate boss. If he does not go through the "chain of command" he endangers his job or career. This chain buffers the top management from things that should be handled elsewhere. However, it also keeps the boss from knowing what really goes on in the heart of his/her organization.

All along the ladder there is mutual distrust and misunderstanding between each sub and his boss. Lack of power of the subs and mutual mistrust between levels create the basis of behaviors which result in ongoing reinforcement of each person's diminished self.

Although the boss can make his sub squirm or do things the sub doesn't wish to do, the sub can partially retaliate by his look, his voice, his behavior or posturing to show his anger or contempt. His retaliation is done in a way which saves his job and may save face. But both superior and subordinate are diminished.

Those who are on the same level often are competitive and therefore trust is minimal. There is often a collusion against the boss which results is some fragile bonding, but in a competitive setting this is weak. In some settings where each member of a group sees no opportunity to go beyond where he is, then the bonding may be sincere and real. In these cases the workers form a support group which protects them from some of the diminishing experiences of those who have no support group.

Even in these cases there is "capping," teasing, and other forms of put-downs between members of the group. This kind of joking is supposed to be "in fun." It is better than the embarrassments which they undergo from their bosses, but it still hurts when it is their turn to be the butt of a joke. It is obvious that this kidding around is a way for members of the group to make themselves feel better at someone else's expense. They can't attack their bosses so they prey on one another. Each can justify his attack by saying, "they do it to me."

In the Air Force one of my close friends was a tall black man. He and I teased each other often. We'd say things to each other and then belly up laughing, but if anyone else dared to put either of our racial or ethnic groups down, he had to be ready to fight. Why? We used one another as buffers against the outside world. Each knew how the majority felt about our groups and by allowing the other to attack in a humorous way, we managed to defuse the pain and anger for a moment.

At work many people are able to do the same thing with those they call their friends. But it is a fragile tightrope even with people who have become honestly close. For those who are merely work acquaintances this is a tightrope from which they often fall. The teased is hurt by the put-down and the teaser becomes scared as he knows there will be some sort of retaliation.

All the above happens even when work relationships are considered good. It happens even with people who have some sort of pride and satisfaction in their work. It happens with people who have control over their jobs, are committed, and have challenging work. However, such teasing and insults mean constant misery and fear for the majority of workers who have jobs which bring them a living and little else. Bashing each other and cathartic put-downs are a way of life for most.

These put-downs are both open and covert. They can focus on how a person does his job, how he dresses or talks, his personal life, or his family, politics, ethnic or religious group.Most of the time the victim hears these comments, but when he doesn't he feels the anger, dislike, hatred, contempt, or fear from his co-workers or bosses. Seldom does a day pass without one or many negative comments penetrating deep into him.

No human being is so thick-skinned that hostile comments can leave him unscathed. My belief is that these constant erosions of a person's self-confidence and self-esteem reinforce the diminished self. This vulnerability is the reason that I say that I have never met a truly secure person.

I've met many well-known, outstanding and creative people, but even they, under deft probing and questioning show a soft belly -- a belly that is constantly exposed like an open wound because it is being opened daily. Hurtfulness is built into our attitudes about work.

If our work is repetitious, dull, and unrewarding, then it is hard for us to convince ourselves that we are important, worthwhile, or significant. A man is asked, "what do you do?" and he is measured by his answer. No amount of therapy or pats on the back can convince him he's worthwhile if his job has little status in the eyes of the majority.

It's worse for a woman. If she is a loving wife and mother and opts to stay home and be a professional wife/mother, she can never escape the constant downward looks, the snide remarks which generalize into the phrase made into a question, "Oh, you're just a housewife?" If she works, there's the feeling that she isn't really doing her job as a parent and/or wife. If she's single or married, but without children, there is the constant, unsubtle insinuation that she is selfish, barren, or in some way unfeminine or unmotherly.

Those men and women who "make it" have done so by sacrificing something. No one makes it without many trade-offs in his dealing with others, his family, and himself.

No one can be a Da Vinci any more. There is too much competition in every field and knowledge grows so rapidly in every discipline that experts become experts in a small part of one discipline. People like the creators of General Systems Theory (an effort to make sense of absolutely everything) have a bewildering breadth of knowledge. Even these unique people can't and don't know everything nor can they also be outstanding in every field. A human must make choices -- to do some things and ignore others. The things he cannot do, he feels insecure and uncertain about.

I have taught all grade levels and most subjects to every conceivable type of child and adult. I've tried most theories and techniques in education, innovated some of my own, and am considered an extraordinary teacher. Yet any first year education student, any citizen from off the street could watch me for one hour and find so many things wrong with my teaching that he could write a book about them. Teaching is very complicated so it's easy to see in retrospect what a teacher could have done. I've videotaped some of what I thought were excellent lessons, but in reviewing them I saw many things I could have done better. Every day when Marie asks me about my day I recall many things I did well, but I also tell her of the things I should have said or done. Yet I am an extraordinarily successful teacher.

Those who are not as educated, sensitive or experienced, what do they think? Many may not be as aware as I am, but no teacher can escape the overt behaviors of his class or the subtle feelings that a child or class sends which tell him he has failed in some ways. No amount of internal, clever psychological defense mechanisms can convince his "guts." He knows his inadequacies just as the most successful innovator knows his.

The workplace exposes each person to his real limitations. He cannot escape making human errors such as those which I've explained in this book. He stands naked, judged by his performance. And, even if he's the best there is, he is never good enough by either his or someone else's standards. There is always uncertainty and insecurity. There is always the assault upon his person which reinforces his diminished self.

What can you do, you who want to create your giant self?

The more you can accept the reality of the insecurities and the fears of those around you as well as your own internal doubts, the more you will be able to define clearly what others are doing to you and you to your self.

I have fought for years to have the necessary powers to define and do my job as I see it. I have suffered much during my struggles, but I have more autonomy than any public school teacher I know or have read about. My giant self is real and built upon a stable structure of knowledge, experience, courage, and successful outcomes. My constant internal doubts are equally real, but my belief that one learns from his mistakes gives me the means to keep learning and to forgive myself. I have thus been enabled to withstand withering criticisms when I have pioneered in new areas.

In a program dealing with at-risk junior high students I am the visionary and creative leader. The other six adults who are teachers, instructional assistants, and a probation officer all have their own roles which each has gradually carved out for him or herself. Usually there is a collegial, democratic atmosphere in which our mutual honesty and trust works. We get angry as well as pleased with one another, but though we may tease or put-down one another, this is increasingly rare and usually gentle. We have created a work environment in which natural disagreements can occur without those involved constantly seething from the real and imagined hurts. (There have been exceptions.)

Not everyone can achieve this at work. Most of you do not have much control over anything except yourself. If you can manage to keep reminding yourself to operate from your giant self rather than your diminished self, you will find yourself actually feeling better. Those around you will find themselves reacting differently to you. They will treat you with more respect and deference because you expect and deserve it.

Begin to notice that when you operate from your giant self you are more competent, more worthwhile, and you deserve better treatment. Remember though, when operating from your giant self you are truly a more effective, productive worker and therefore deserving of respect. It has been earned by your deeds.

Twenty-Six

Government and Your Diminished Self

The best government is no government. Democracy is the worst possible government, except when you compare it with all the others. These are paraphrases of famous quotes about government and express most people's views of the intrusive role their government plays in their lives.

The government you love or admire generally is the only one you know about. People are happy or unhappy under all kinds of rulers and leaders who don't seem to have their subjects' best interests at heart. What is known about the brain indicates that a person's choice of government may also reflect his learning style and how he organizes his world. With others, it is their status, how much of the pie that they get to share that determines their choice of government.

When you get to the nitty-gritty, most people don't choose their government; it is imposed upon them. And despite their complaints, most people feel impotent against its power. Most citizens are realistically afraid of governmental powers and this is a major source of their diminished self.

For those who live under a dictatorship, a military oligarchy, or any of the forms of socialism or communism which are basically totalitarian regimes, there is very little they can do to change the government or to increase their personal liberties. World opinion, economic, social, and political forces sometimes shape the conditions in which one person may be a catalyst or a symbol for evolutionary changes, but if that person is too far ahead of his time he will either be killed or ignored.

Myths about how great men have changed the course of history are used to convince you that you also possess great power and the capability to change history alone. It's true that gifted, creative, and unusual humans have led the way in every step of human and social evolution, but most discoveries were also made by other individuals at approximately the same time. I do not wish to denigrate or downplay the effort or greatness of any person who has contributed to progress, but merely to put the possibilities of your doing so in a realistic perspective.

Activating, encouraging the growth of your giant self means realistically assessing your potentials and opportunities. That's why "fighting city hall," should be done with full knowledge of who and what you're fighting and appraising how much you should attempt and how much you want to risk. As a person who has fought "city hall" many times, I always advise others to do so with their eyes wide open. I tell them the odds against making any changes, the risks involved, the emotional traumas, and advise them to make certain they can handle the fear, pain, and rejection which usually comes with the territory. I also point out that when I have been successful, it was worth all the times I wasn't. As long as people know the price and the trade-offs, they can act accordingly.

The government is based on rules of law that go back to Mosaic, then Roman, then English law. The Constitution and Bill of Rights contain some of the most ethical and moral concepts in political thought and practice. We don't follow them as we should, but they are guides which have elevated us beyond any other large government in history. Still, even though they protect us from political forces better than any other documents, they include laws which prohibit our freedoms in many ways.

When federal state or local laws infringe upon what you and I wish to do, we want them modified or revoked. At least under our form of government, changing the law is possibility although it is time-consuming and often takes a great deal of money and organizational ability. However, it can be done.

If it is to be done it also means fighting the lethargy, inertia, and indifference inherent in any kind of bureaucracy. The best way to deal with government workers is to recognize that they are functioning from their diminished selves. If you meet them with your giant self and are not distressed by the games they must play to overcome the put-downs they constantly experience, then you can help and encourage them to function from their giant selves. They then become your partners and change becomes a possibility. This does not mean kissing their butts, but respecting them as valuable humans. By talking to bureaucrats as if they were a combination of your best friend and someone you feared but admired, you would be treating them in a way that could get the same treatment from them.

By facing the realities of government bureaucracy, you can manage to live within the reasonable limits imposed upon you by government. You are still free to fight for the slow but possible and reasonable changes that can be made by an informed and enlightened citizen acting from his giant self.

Government and bureaucracy are great intimidators and can make you feel vulnerable, afraid, and child-like. After all, besides serving the public, they must protect it. Most of the time bureaucrats believe that they are protecting the country and at the some time are doing things for "your own good." They sincerely believe they are doing the right thing even though the damage they are doing and the pain they are inflicting upon you is real.

People who work for the government will take your questions and statements as a challenge to our country -- and themselves. Your task is to make them aware that the changes you request are not meant to belittle or challenge them or impose blame upon them. Also, that helping to improve anything does not mean the way things were was bad. This is critical if you are to budge most of them. They should be made to feel that they were doing their jobs well, it's just that there is new information causing a different situation and that a new solution or perspective is needed. Help them understand how your need or solution will improve their job and those whom they serve. And be patient as well as persistent, because changes in a democracy are often interdependent upon complex relationships and they take time. Finding and learning who and what is involved will insure your success and speed up the process of change.

Growth and development are dependent upon minds which can adapt to new situations and settings. It is not a matter of being a con-artist or manipulator, but of expressing your giant self.

Part Three

Creating Your Giant Self

Twenty-Seven

Long Term Relationships: Marriage

This chapter is pivotal. It could just as easily have been placed in the section dealing with the institutions of society and how they, more often then not, increase your negative feelings about yourself, that is, how they butcher your self-confidence and diminish you. Even though long-term relationships, especially the ones that include sexual relationships, are frequently disastrous to your giant self, they have the greatest potential to enhance it. Therefore, this chapter will begin with the ways long-term relationships cause you to see yourself from your diminished self, but then it will lead into the last part of this book which will explain how these relationships are the keys to your giant self.

Every human being can be better understood if you see him/her as totally selfish. No matter how he disguises his behavior, every person wants his own way. He wants whatever and whomever can satisfy his real and believed needs and desires and he will try anything to get them.

This places a person into direct conflict with his social institutions which are concerned with the welfare of the group or species and not with him as an individual. At the same time society must meet enough of his needs to get or keep his loyalty. I've spent most of the book describing these conflicts.

The institutions of a society try to train a person to act less selfishly. To the degree they are successful they provide the key to his comfortably compromising or modifying his needs and desires to fit into the greater communal good. A person is considered dangerous if his wants cause harm to others or to the group. He is considered deviant if his behavior is too different from others and moreover seems to hurt him. He is creative if his behavior is considered deviant or dangerous, but proves to be of benefit to the group.

A further complication arises when people from many different subcultures meet and must adapt to one another. What one person or group considers deviant, dangerous, or just different may be considered a personal or social good by others. In relationships the same individual may be different from his partner is some important ways, but he is sympatico, very much in tune, in many others.

Example: Homosexuality and bisexuality may be creative ways to deal with sex; they may be somewhat different ways to satisfy sexual urges which the majority considers deviant. With the spread of AIDS they may pose dangerous problems affecting the majority. The financial cost of AIDS is borne by everyone although only a small percentage of the population were making independent choices.

Gang members are making choices which they should have the constitutional right to make. That is, they should be allowed to meet with and be with whomever they wish. However, their behaviors, especially drug dealing and inter-gang conflicts endanger the lives of many other non gang members and cause financial costs to their communities.

A spouse who chooses to have other relations is asserting her right to do whatever she wishes with her body. However, the emotional pain which often occurs to her spouse affects many more people than herself.

We are trapped between the apparent guarantees of our constitution to allow an individual the rights to satisfy his selfish needs and the obvious damage to others when, in the process of meeting his needs, a person overtly or inadvertently hurts others.

I'll start with a long-term relationship which has the best chances of surviving and explore the factors which complicate and make relationships increasingly less successful.

Before you accuse me of perversity, hear me out. I am not advocating anything but applying a consistent frame of reference and logic. The most enduring long-term relationships would be those in which the two people share some similar backgrounds, goals, and many commonalties. Therefore the relationship of a man with a man, a woman with a woman would seem to have the greatest statistical chance of success. Except if they engage in sex. Sex changes it all because of the emotional forces it unleashes. Nonsexual homosexual relationships between people who have much in common and love one another have the potential of lifetime commitment.

My two closest friends are people I have been close to since I was a teenager forty plus years ago. They are still loved by me. A third friend, despite my efforts to close a serious breach, has ended our communications. I have not given up on him though. There have never been any overt homosexual feelings involved between any of us nor any bisexual experiences. We are all from a traditional Jewish background, but we have dealt with our heritage very differently. I rejected Judaism the earliest and the most violently and have been the most radical and creative.

However, each can understand and appreciate the forces which caused him to cope with Judaism differently. We are all teachers. One has gone into administration, a second became a college professor, and the other is also a lawyer. Each has far surpassed his father in education and income, but his relationship with his father has been a lifelong problem and open wound. Only one has maintained a lifetime relationship with his first love. He is also the only one who still practices his religion. The rest have divorced and remarried non-Jewish women.

We all have nice homes, mine being the most modest since my income is less than theirs. I am the only one with a one-income family and I have the most children. I believe that among the group that Marie is the most successful mother and I think I am considered the best father.

Our families were all white Europeans with all the values, emotions, and practices each brought to America. Politically, we all began as Democrats as well as with a deep belief in monogamy. Why place monogamy with politics? Because it is as much a political stance as it is a psycho-social one. The three of us that dealt with divorce, family break-up, and loss of our children had many forces acting upon us which increased the trauma. We shared these.

All of these commonalties have enabled our friendship to survive many unique and different experiences which would have destroyed it had we not had so many shared values, beliefs, and experiences. I could easily have lived happily with any one of these friends all of my life, because we are very compatible. However, I wanted a wife and children and so did they. Because we were so similar in important ways and didn't have the personal complications and powerful emotions sex brings we could have had fairly conflict-free relationships.

If one of us had been a Christian, a non-European, of a different race or ethnic group, less educated and bright, this difference would have added to the forces which sometimes break up friendships. I am not saying a lifetime friendship or relationship cannot occur with these differences because it can. Two friends I met while I was in the Air Force have endured almost forty years. One was a Ghanian whom I lived with at various times. We learned much about our different cultures and our friendship broadened our lives. The other was a Catholic while I was a Jew. He was one of the most brilliant men I've ever know. He has the capacity to make complex ideas and theories simple. He taught me more philosophy and linguistics than my professors.

These two have lived great distances from me which diluted the intensity of our relationships. All in all I have been fortunate to be blessed with these men as lifelong friends. No woman friend, except Marie, has stood the test of time as these men have. Why?

Because despite my poetic phrases to the contrary, it is difficult for a woman to understand a man as well as another man can. I think it is better to see the two sexes as if they are two different species. A woman writing this could substitute her female friends for my male ones. I also believe that if we think of these differences as species differences, without any sense of one being superior to the other then we will work harder in adjusting to these differences!

Of course there are those who make a strong case for these differences being merely the result of past injustices towards women by physically stronger men. These people feel that women have been historically derogated to subordinate roles because they bear children. The child's dependency on the mother prenatally and after birth has also forced the mother to be dependent upon the father because pregnancy and breast-feeding limits her in time and space more than it does the father.

Man started as the freer one who could go out and do the hunting, which was more dangerous than staying in camp nurturing the young and foraging for food. However, his greater musculature and physical strength is not cultural but is a physical fact. Granted, some women now are faster and stronger than the majority of men, but these are the exceptions.

Observing other species you see the physically weaker developing patterns of behavior to get what they want form the stronger. Usually there is some type of fawning, begging, or obsequiousness on the part of the weaker. The stronger usually gives the weaker his scraps or gives in temporarily when he wants to mate. And, very few animals mate for life. Most mate briefly and then if there is any care given to their young it is the females who provide it. The males go their own way. In some species the male mates with many females and protects his harem from other males. Even highly civilized human societies have allowed one male, a chief, sheik, or king to have more than one mate while in animal and human societies it is a rarity for a female to have more than one mate.

Monogamy is obviously not the will of a god or he/she would have built monogamy into the human brain and physiology. Polygamy is because it maximizes the species survival. In fact, monogamy is a social creation to insure a more equitable distribution of property. Marriage is the social and political means to ritualize this property distribution and make it legally binding, said property being women and commodities they produce -- children. Having written this I may have to retreat to Antarctica.

Social creations such as private property (thou shalt not steal), respecting and caring for your parents (thou shalt honor thy father and mother), and not murdering your neighbors for their property (thou shalt not kill) were not made by the strong because they simply took what they wanted. These were made by the weaker members of society (the meek shall inherit the earth -- of course, there's more of them) because they were getting screwed, but not getting any sex. The strong were getting all the intelligent, beautiful women and the weak were banging themselves, each other, or closing their eyes while sharing the unwanted ones.

I contend that this seeming inequity was built into human physiology. It was not a question of right or wrong, it was the nature of the beast. And, it made good species sense. If in nature the species is more important than any one individual and this seems a reasonable belief, then whatever increases the species' survival is what is built into its DNA, its genetic code, its physiological nature.

It makes good species sense for the healthiest, the best examples of survival to breed with each other. It makes good sense for the weakest not to breed because they produce those who will become most burdensome on the rest. This was why many so-called primitives killed the handicapped at birth.

I fully realize that this is the logic that Hitler and every racist, sexist, and pervert uses to justify the belief in his inherent superiority and the genetic inferiority of his victims. Then he can take whatever he can and not feel guilty. I stand by my statements because I believe they are true.

I stand by my statement that women and men are, by nature, very different physiologically and this does not just mean the obvious differences in plumbing. I believe each sex's internal chemistry causes it to see the world in a qualitatively different way. This different way of seeing is built into the DNA. However, I repeat, there should be no inferences about one being superior to the other. Each has unique qualities that the other also has but not to the some degree. Because of these differences it is very difficult for men and women to see or feel things the same way and this causes constant friction.

The strong have always gotten their unfair share. However, there were those who, when man was hunting, then farming, then industrializing, gradually fought for more equal distribution of whatever resources were available.

The unequal distribution of wealth still exists, but monogamy is no longer a rarity, it is the new reality. With science advancing as it has, those who were considered the weak and who would not have been allowed to live, certainly not to mate, are kept alive and even mate.

Stephen Hawking, one of the greatest scientists of this century has had from birth a crippling disease which keeps him in a wheel chair. He can barely communicate. But what he has contributed to his species gives notice that the old conception of what is good for the species is deeply in question. Many parents with children with Downs Syndrome feel they have not been punished, but have been truly blessed to have a child who loves so deeply. Many people with major and minor handicaps contribute to their societies and families. In times past they would have been killed or died at birth or soon after.

Without bringing a god into the equation, man has been the victim of his physiology and so has created societies and institutions which reflect his genetic givens. Polygamy was an example of this dominance of some over others. Rich people flourishing at the expense of the poor and consciously creating poverty by their manipulation of capital, goods, and services is another.

Monogamy and other efforts to more fairly distribute the world's natural resources are examples of evolutionary steps forward. We are on the verge of manipulating our DNA, our genetic givens, without the time constraints of Mendelian genetics. We may soon be able to change our physiological tendencies to a higher level of functioning. I consider equality, justice, and love higher order behavior than selfishly (slavishly) following our physiology.

If you apply evolutionary thinking to monogamy/marriages, then marriage is elevated from a thoughtless, sexually satisfying, child-breeding social vehicle to one in which two different humans with many commonalties but many other, hopefully complementary needs and functions get together to spend a lifetime in potentiating and actualizing their giant selves.

A slight digression to strengthen my case: If you step on any school playground you will see an enormous range of behaviors. If you questioned each set of children who were in a fight you would see a bewildering difference in the causes of the fight, the individual complex motivations, intelligence, and maturity levels. Yet in most schools there are strict rules and penalties for fighting. I contend that if those rules were rigidly followed there would be great injustice and the combatants would not profit from consequences of their actions.

I treated each fight as if it were a constitutional case. Each child had his day in court, a chance to explain his side, as well as to help me to understand his motives. I have paddled them, even paddled those who watched because I believe most fights would not get to a physical level if there were not the mob cheering it on. Others I have tried in our student courts because I felt the students saw me as arbitrary and unfair, but a trial by their peers satisfied them. Some offenders I suspended because paddling them would only worsen their inclination to physical punishment. Some I counseled and they responded so well they became my aides in preventing other fights. Some I merely held and stroked because that's what they needed, not words or punishments. My expertise was in knowing when to do what to whom.

The same applies to the delicate balancing necessary between any two humans, but more so when they are of the opposite sex. I do not foresee monogamy as the only way to satisfy human isolation, sexuality, or child rearing. Just as each child on the playground needs to be treated differently if he is to create his giant self, so each person in a relationship needs to find the ways that best allow each to grow.

Although I believe monogamy has the greatest potential for humans to create their giant selves, I don't believe we should fear or stop other groupings which consenting adults choose. Those who knowingly and willingly enter into bigamy, polygamy, communal marriages or just one or more couples living together so they can afford housing should not only be legally allowed, these arrangements need to applauded for their courage and creativity. Those involved in such alternatives should have the same legal protections the state provides for a monogamous relationship.

On an evolutionary basis I approve of intermarriage and inter-relationships between people of different religious, racial and ethnic backgrounds. This kind of mixing enriches the species' gene pool and potentiates the species' problem-solving capacities which is critical for solving the problems of the future. The same logic applies to legalizing any long-term voluntary human relationships, no matter how different they are from the accepted norm. These unique couplings or groupings, like intermarriages, have the potential of helping us understand more of what we are genetically as opposed to who we become through socialization and programming.

Those living outside the norm will find that the same kinds of human errors I've spoken of will need to be faced as well as all the intrusions of the various social institutions. However, if we could accept that one man's heaven is another's hell and let him find his own way without our interferences or moralizing (or law-making and punishments, unless his own way poses a serious danger to himself, partner(s) or others), most people would evolve to higher levels of morality and ethics.

I have read extensively, thought of the consequences, acted upon my beliefs, and agonized over the conflicts which monogamy brings. I have concluded that it is the best vehicle for our species evolution. It is not easy because two people committed only to one another pose many problems and burdens for each other. It takes two people willing to devote much time and energy to the project. The obstacles are overwhelming. Yet, the possible results are emotionally and spiritually rewarding in that they and their family have a means to experience and express love in ennobling ways that no other man-made creation offers. There is specialness, a respect for the other that only happens in a lifetime of monogamy.

Yes, I have purposely left out a god because I believe that a marriage can be an evolutionary worthwhile experience without depending upon a god. However, I would not exclude a god from a marriage if it would help the partners create their giant selves.

I have barely mentioned sex for the same reason. A good marriage and/or relationship can exist with little or no sex. (I know of good marriages with little sex, but such an arrangement is not for me. I am too insecure and sex temporarily helps me alleviate my fears.) I have read and I can intellectually appreciate how an increase in spirituality could decrease the dependency on sex. For whatever the reasons I do not wish to follow that path. I meditate and believe this practice increases my spirituality.

Whether my attitude toward these matters is a rationalization to retain my full-blooded sexuality I do not know. I believe in balance and trade-offs. I think a person who gives up his sexuality for spirituality is no healthier than one who gives up a spiritual life for sex. Neither is a fully developed person because he is denying a part of himself.

For the purposes of this book I am assuming that monogamy (in the same way I believe in the Constitution as the best means for political justice) is the best vehicle for equality and justice within a human relationship. I know it is an arguable point because I have agonized about it most of my life, but monogamy is a man-made structure which can be modified to fit our increasing knowledge of the mind/body. If you wish to bring a god into it I would not object if that's your belief, your style, or your level of evolution.

I would strongly object if you tried to force a god into my marriage or relationship just because you needed one. One of the main goals of this book has been to raise the level of toleration for ideas and people different from you or me. I hope that there can be a flourishing of attempts to discover how much of our relationships are based on genetics, how much on man-made socially created institutions, and how much on the interactions between them. This can not occur when we condemn others for acting in ways which do not conform to our own unique, individual, genetic-social programming. I may not approve of two people of the same sex living together as mates, two of the opposite sex who do not engage in sex, or those living in communal arrangements different from my monogamous one. However, as long as they don't force me to do as they do, I should not attempt to pass laws preventing their means to find the human relationships which creates their giant selves.

From this attitude will come the data to determine what is human and what is aberrant. Presently, it seems to me, it is more human to be in a monogamous relationship. It is also more complex and difficult than short-term, serial relationships. It is a question of trade-offs and how giant you want your giant self to become.

Although the rest of the book will deal with how to create your giant self within marriage and one-on-one relationships, the concepts should help those on other levels of their evolution to form whatever relationships they wish for their mutual needs.

Twenty-Eight

Getting Into Other People's Realities

The American Indian concept of walking a month in another person's shoes before judging them succinctly explains this chapter.

Twenty-Nine

Hope, the Eternal Spring

The saying that hope springs eternal in the hearts of men is more than a popular expression. The statement is a guide for healthy, productive living. Hope may frequently seem irrational, illogical and to an outside observer even blatantly stupid. For that matter the same could be said of religion, love or any other strongly felt emotional state.

Both planning and hope are essential to creating a better life, but there is a significant difference between them. When you are thinking about your future in a completely rational way that is a plan, not hope. Hope is a way you deal with real and imagined fears and also a way you energize yourself toward your goals and desires.

Hope keeps your personal realities alive. Don't let those who are operating from their diminished selves diminish you or demolish your hopes, however much they may try. Your hopes are your personal property. Hope may not make all your desires come to pass but without hope it is unlikely that any of them will. Hope is crucial to creating your giant self and making the best life you can.

How do you decide whether hope or cold logic should be applied to a specific situation? I spoke earlier about the validity of intuition and compared its value to logic. I mentioned that each has its strengths and weaknesses and that neither is applicable to all situations. The same is true of hope. As to when hope is the appropriate response to a situation I know you would like to have a formula which you could apply to any dilemma but I can't give you one. The decision is yours and anyone who says he can give you a simple formula telling you what you should or should not hope for is either wrong headed or out to make a buck at your expense.

I have found that by refusing to surrender my private hopes in the face of all kinds of negative reaction, discouragement and even scorn I have experienced many personal fulfillments. These would have been impossible without keeping alive the initial, apparently unrealistic hope that preceded them. I confess I had youthful thoughts of a Nobel Prize in Literature when I submitted my first story to a famous magazine -- a story hand written in green ink on lined school paper. In spite of all indications, dissuasions and probabilities I have finally had books published, plays produced, created and controlled my own educational program which has benefited thousands and in addition gained many other rewards. Hard work was necessary but hope was the crucial ingredient; none of these things would have happened without it. Operating from your giant self makes it possible not only to work for your hopes but to endure and survive the disappointments and frustrations along the way.

Hope can be a gentle tug or a sharp reminder of unlimited possibilities. Hope is not infallible, of course. It is subject to error just as logic or intuition are. Be aware that your present hope may lead you into grievous pain or be a way to your personal promised land. Either way it is invaluable. Hope nourishes the images of a better future which sustain us when life is almost too difficult to bear. Hope makes growth toward your giant self possible.

An intensely hopeful person usually can't explain his hopes to other people. All too often their first impulse is to laugh or to throw cold water on his dreams. The diminishers are smug because they have used logic to poke holes in the hopeful one's weak arguments on behalf of his hopes. It is helpful to perceive the dynamics which are going on in this kind of encounter.

The average person thinks of his future in terms of what others believe is valuable. The hopeful person projects himself forward in terms of his deeply felt and very personal view of his own realities. Each finds it virtually impossible to communicate his viewpoint convincingly. They are arguing from different realities, neither one necessarily superior or inferior to the other. The man with hope may be misguided but on the other hand he may be speaking from his giant self with the confidence of one who sees a vision of a better world, a more interesting world. The person with a purely logical perspective may not be able to see this kind of future at all. He is literally not in a position to see it.

If your hope gives you the necessary strength, courage and will to improve your life in a way that does not hurt others then you must not let individuals operating from their diminished selves talk you out of it. This does not mean mortgaging your home and your family's future for some scheme presented by a clever crook appealing to your ego. If you fell in with something like that you would be operating from your diminished and not your giant self.

Hope is the basis of all religions. Since time began man has feared a life without meaning and a death which meant oblivion. The hope of a better life here on earth and of an afterlife elsewhere has kept the majority of mankind reasonably sane.

Many people today stop hoping and live out their lives as faceless mediocrities or worse. They may try to bury their despair in the endless array of addictions available to those who live without hope.

You chose this book because you hoped it would help you to become more than you are. It will, but only if you persevere in your hope. Your giant self is built upon hope. Hope on.

Thirty

Risks, Baby Steps Giant Strides

Hope is wonderful, marvelous, and gives you the strength to persevere. However, if you want to overcome your fears, your diminished self, and create your giant self you must take risks. Risk is the conscious physical acting out, the actualization of you hopes, your dreams and your fantasies. Rick separates the idle dreamer from the successful (and unsuccessful) doer of deeds.

In commodities, the stock market, and business in general, those who take the greatest risks make (and lose) the most money. As in business so it is in life, the greatest risks give the greatest pay-offs (and losses).

I had the chance to go kayaking with a friend. I had always been fascinated with kayaks as used by the Eskimos. My friend showed me where he kayaked and it looked like fun. Before I realized it I had said we should go immediately while I was excited and not yet fearful. He took me up on it and in a little while we were carrying kayaks towards the ocean. Marie says kindly that I have a healthy fear of the ocean. No; it scares me, but I swim anyway. I'm a good swimmer, but as we neared the waves I was fighting my fears. The worst thing that could happen was that I'd tip over, fall out, and make an ass out of myself. My friend had said that there was an easy way to right yourself when you tipped over, but I did not find that comforting. I followed him in and had a great experience. I had calculated the risks and decided it was worth it and I was right. I was glad I took the risk.

When Marie and I met, fell in love, and wanted to get married we were constantly hassled by our ex's. I knew if we remained in L.A. they'd drive us crazy and possibly ruin our relationship. At the time I was very secure in that I was a tenured teacher during the school year and a L.A. County Deputy Probation Officer during the summer. I had completed my course work for an M.A. in psychology and had passed two of my four comprehensive exams. I had even completed my first novel. I had a New York agent who was excited about my talent and was eager to receive the second novel which I was writing. My life was totally set, comfortable, and full of promise. I was thirty.

I gave up all my security and comforts because I loved Marie. I left it all in a wildly romantic, love-intoxicated mania with the woman I loved passionately. I took an enormous risk that I could make it as a writer right then. We sold everything and flew to Puerto Rico. We stayed two days and flew to Santa Barbara. We were living on my retirement pay which ran out while I was trying to make a living writing. I risked everything and lost. But, I was with Marie, which made it all worthwhile.

At eighteen I had the chance to train to be an Olympic athlete. Instead of training I stayed out night after night and tried to set an Olympic record for orgasms. I risked and made my choice. Unfortunately, my orgasm record was unofficial and no scholarships or public recognition followed from my exploits.

At twenty I gave up being a conscientious objector because if I hadn't I wouldn't have been allowed to marry Isabel, my first wife, I chose love and Isabel.

In each case I went against logic, everyone's advise, and flowed with my heart. I risked and lost much, but also gained much. What I gained was not always evident for a long time.

When Marie and I began multi-level marketing I did a lot of financial juggling and was scared. Most of our endeavor did not work out as we hoped, but we learned from it. I ended up with an additional doctorate (nutrition) and we knew how to run a business. If I died she had many more marketable skills. Most importantly, we learned much more about healthful living and this has paid great dividends for us, our family, and our friends.

In education I have constantly risked my career and reputation by teaching in non-traditional ways and doing things that were before their time and unpopular. My unconventional approach placed me in an unpopular light so I lost summer teaching jobs, consultant positions, and was told that I could apply all I wanted but I would never be selected to be a principal. I lost money, but I gained in self-respect. How many people can look at themselves in the mirror without wishing they'd said or did something which they hadn't? I almost always did what my conscience dictated and what I believed was best for children, their parents, or teachers. Ironically, most of the things I stood and fought for later became accepted practices, but by then I was at another plateau so I never received public recognition.

When others wish to try their sea legs and go from baby steps to the giant strides of their giant selves, I caution them. I have the kind of personalty, character, and self-confidence which enables me to stand alone. Many times I have had people tell me they would stand behind me, but when the risks became evident I found them behind me in their prayers but not in their bodies.

I can appreciate race-car drivers, soldiers of fortune, financiers, and creative minds of all kinds as they risk their lives and careers by boldly stepping into the unknown. It is a heady feeling and whether you win or lose, you always gain because the process, the experience itself is worth it all. However, such daring is not for everyone.

I remind people that I have, from everyone else's viewpoint, lost more battles than I've won. Can they stand up to the feelings and fears that losing normally brings? Can they take the looks, the snide remarks overheard, and the other kinds of rejections which come from asserting their giant selves? I tell them that most creative people or change agents also possess a specific body of knowledge and skills which they can use to argue, prove their point, and to produce a product. I discourage them. If they give up, they weren't ready. If they decide to go ahead, I counsel preparedness -- and hope.

In the end each man has to wrestle alone with his fears and demons. Each has to decide how much he is willing to risk (and lose) to achieve something he holds dear or wishes to discover or experience.

If the adventurous man is not frightened because of the risks involves, then he is either a fool or self-destructive. In each case there should be a willingness to assess the risks, the dangers, and the disadvantages, as well as the believed advantages, I have no respect for the man who has not calculated his risks. The healthy risk-taker, the person acting from his giant self, has done his homework and has researched the risks to the best of his ability. He is fearful, but he acts courageously, not allowing his fears to dictate his actions.

The man who is unafraid is not courageous. A courageous individual is the person who is afraid, but takes the risk anyway. Stupidity is not an attribute of the risk-taker.

Obviously I believe your growth is based on taking calculated risks. I do not think human growth is possible without risks. However, I reemphasize the absolute importance of preparation. Study every conceivable angle to make certain you have minimized your risks.

A stunt man purposely wants his stunts to look as dangerous as possible. The professionals in this field who are most long-lived are those who carefully calculate their risks and seldom take unnecessary ones. They mix knowledge, skill, and courage.

The same should be true for you. Growth is absolutely dependent on risk. Still, minimize your risks by using logical thinking, intuition, or other data-gathering devices. Examine the trade-offs. Talk to others. Pray if that works for you. Meditate. When you've done everything you can think of, then (if you still want to go with your venture), follow your heart and guts and take the risk.

I've warned you and I shall repeat that there is no certainty, no guarantee in anything, no matter how well-prepared and informed you are or think you are. No one can possibly know all the consequences or outcomes of any course of action. If there were certainty, there wouldn't be any risk.

Life is a constant risk. I love it. It scares me, but I love it.

So, be well-prepared, but recognize that there will be risks whatever you choose. And, not choosing is also a choice. The growth of your giant self is dependent on the number and kinds of risks you take -- and what you learn from them. Remember all the ways you can make errors, how you are controlled by your social institutions and specific people, and then stand tall, take your lumps and risks, and live your life. Full steam ahead!

Thirty-One

All God's Children Got Rhythm

One stereotype is that all Black people can dance because they all have rhythm. When I first studied what was then Negro History I was attempting to disprove the stereotype believing that this would reduce prejudice. What I found was that in most of Africa dance was an integral part of each tribe's religious and social ceremonies. Literally, everyone had to dance. The next issue that presented itself; which Africans were selected as slaves and which ones survived the incredible human deprivations of the passage across the ocean from Africa to the Americas? The answer was those who were the best physical specimens. The next hurdle was the difficult life on the plantations. Finally, the healthiest, strongest, and brightest (because slaves weren't just used for labor, but were the skilled tradesmen) were used for breeding. Take genetic givens plus social conditioning and you get a lot of people who can dance.

Dance is just one means of expressing human rhythm. Almost all Chinese have rhythm. Why? Each morning in China, millions of people, alone or in large groups practice a stretching, strengthening rhythmic body discipline.

The opposite of the powerful drumming beats of the Africans, Tai Chi is a quiet, peaceful, slow moving exercise in controlled gracefulness and strength.

In many European countries, especially under the influence of religious leaders who taught their people to fear the rhythms (especially sexual) of their bodies, people believed dancing was an expression of the devil. It is easy to see why these people saw the Africans, who were merely expressing their religious beliefs by dancing, as heathens, devil-worshipers, and subhuman. With this belief it was easy to create stereotypes about the Blacks which gave the Europeans what they believed was a God-given right to treat Africans as they would any other farm or domesticated animal.

Whenever we generalize about any group, there is a kernel of truth about them based on the various facts and the way we interpret them. Since the brain is a pattern detector it is necessary for us to give, even force, some meaning to our observations. The rhythms of each group are real. Look at the complex rhythms in a modern society. The majority of people live in a nine to five rhythm with short breaks for excretory functions and longer ones for eating. In order for the majority to work during this time-span another large percentage has to work at different times, within different rhythms, to produce, transport, and prepare the food and other raw materials for the nine to fivers.

No matter what work rhythm a person must follow his body has to adjust to it if he is to remain healthy. The reality is that many people are in jobs where their unique individual rhythms do not fit physiologically or psychologically into the group rhythms. The result is minor and major physiological and psychological illnesses. These cause minor to major perturbations in the rhythms of the group.

The fact that many children can not physiologically function at their best in the early morning and reading is traditionally taught then means that the group rhythm of the school guarantees a large percentage of children will not be successful readers.

The reality of life is that group rhythms are set up for efficiency and do not take into consideration the unique rhythms of its individual members. The person either adjusts or suffers the consequences. Many teachers, who are as limited by the time frames as are the students, are unable to train their bowels to operate on these schedules with resulting hemorrhoids, flatulence, and other uncomfortable or serious bladder, kidney, stomach, intestinal, or colon problems.

I am not saying that everyone who adjusts to group rhythms suffers some dire consequences, because the schedule is often based on a majority consensus. Most people can adjust their rhythms to nine to five and most teachers and students have no problem regulating their bodily systems to the requirements of the group rhythm. In fact, as research has shown about girls in a dorm, often each one's unique menstrual period gradually coincides until the majority are menstruating on the same schedule. These sorts of things happen between all animals and come from the combination of physiological and social signals.

To actualize your giant self you must be able to understand the rhythms of the groups you are in as well as your own unique ones. You must be able to make the adjustments to maximize your abilities while minimizing your disruptions within each group. Or, you must be willing, as creative people are, to endure the negativity of those you are trying to change while leading them into new rhythms and structures. These are trade-offs only you can determine.

For some of you, once you have realized that your rhythms cannot fit into a setting you are in, you must find another more compatible. My ex-wife is very unfriendly until she has her morning coffee, but I am full of energy and ready to go as soon as my eyes open. We irritated each other constantly. Marie is like me and we start each day in good spirits. It wasn't that I didn't love Isabel or vice-versa, but our rhythms and values were too different for us to be willing or able to adjust to each other even though we both made valiant efforts.

Since I have had classroom aides and have been able to leave the room according to my rhythms I have been more comfortable and healthier. If you cannot adjust your bodily rhythms to the group rhythms you need either to negotiate with your boss or get another job. Easy to say, difficult to do, but the change could make you much healthier, happier, and more effective. What makes this issue more complex is that your individual rhythms may vary slightly to greatly. And they are affected by stress, others' rhythms, and factors such as diet, sleep, and exercise. (I didn't promise you a rose garden. Creating your giant self is a life-long, complicated task.)

Besides learning about and understanding your bodily rhythms such as eating, sleeping, energy patterns, excretory functions, and intellectual abilities, you should realize how all these interact and affect one another. In fact your immune system seems to have a mind of its own as well as being dependent on all other systems. Complex behaviors stemming from your sexual, social, or spiritual needs are also interactive and interdependent.

Everything you do is the result of various physically and socially induced and structured rhythms and usually you are minimally aware of them. A person who does anything which is not in synch with his or her groups' rhythms suffers in some ways. A man who (on the social level) cheats his neighbors and gets away with it may well get his punishment (on the spiritual level) by either the guilt he feels or, if he evades his guilt, by the erosion of his character.

Throughout the book I have explained how people and institutions diminish you by not allowing you to express your unique rhythms. Obviously, in a society every person cannot do whatever he wants whenever he wants, but if a person totally capitulates to social demands at the expense of his rhythms he will not be a valuable addition to his group. Therefore, to insure the creative development of your giant self you need to be able to honestly appraise and understand your rhythms, examine how they fit within your groups, and then either modify yours or the groups' rhythms, or find settings more compatible.

In schools, which restrict the expression of individual rhythms, I have found many ways to safely and productively allow my students and myself to follow our rhythms by making slight modifications of patterns which many believed would cause great disturbances within the institution. Allowing even first graders the unlimited privilege of getting water or going to the lavatory whenever they wanted, but one at a time, seldom caused any problems. Instead of chaos, there was an increase in order and mutual respect.

Many of our social patterns were imposed upon us by those with greater power who were disinterested in individual rhythms. They alleged this was for the good of the majority which usually translated into being good for their individual profit or benefit.

Learn your rhythms. Learn the rhythm of your groups. Harmony means that you and those around you either naturally or through learning can move to the same rhythms. The girls in the dorm, the freedom my students and I share, a marching band, and a factory assembly line in which each person feels fulfilled are examples of learned rhythms.

The creation of your giant self is a conscious learning, understanding, flowing, and modifying of your individual and group rhythms. One very complex issue is that of your sexual rhythms which are examined next.

Thirty-Two

Sex: Variations on a Theme

Years ago I wrote a long article exploring the evolution of sexuality from the rhythms of one-celled animals to man. I was trying to determine what was "natural" sexual behavior and what was determined by culture -- the nature-nurture controversy. Like many people today I realized that any either/or questions results in answers that are limiting. My conclusion was that man is controlled by neither nature or nurture alone, but his choices are the result of the interactions of these two powerful rhythms as well a his own conscious will.

You are born with many genetic givens, physiological potentials, with which you interact within your social/cultural environments. There are always elements of conscious choice. You may choose abstinence, promiscuity, or any position in between. I will suggest some ways to look at different sexual purposes and rhythms.

Reproductive sex: Every cell, organ, and system in your body serves one or more biological purposes. Your sexual-reproductive system is an example. Its primary purpose is to serve your species, not you. In all living things the individual organism has its moment in time; then it makes way for the next generation by its death. This is hard for man to accept, so he doesn't. He creates beliefs to counter his mortality.

Through reproductive sex he can achieve a kind of immortality. He can live forever because some of the genes of the earliest humans still are active in a man's gene pool. The more women he impregnates, the more children who survive, the more of him will survive in some form. Therefore whether this is realized consciously or in some kind of consensual resonance, one of the most powerful driving forces for each person is reproductive sex to insure this immortality wish.

Recreational sex: We tend to attribute to animal behavior thoughts, feelings, and behaviors which we possess. Reproductive sex makes sense for animals, but why do they engage in recreational sex? Dolphins and apes seem to indulge in sex as a form of play. Do they have similar pleasurable feelings to those we enjoy? In animals is their sexual play just practice for reproduction? In adults, if mating is not their goal, are they just screwing around?

Young humans engage in all sorts of sexual play that is quickly stopped if observed by jealous adults. Since their hormones are not turned on or tuned in, what are they getting from pre-coital play? If it will make them better at reproductive sex, should we allow it to occur? At what point does sex stop being practice for reproduction (good for the species) and become recreational (good for the practioners?)

Without the social taboos, the fears imposed upon individuals by their cultures, the young would explore their bodies and discover the pleasures of their genitals, mouth, and rectum. They would touch, hug, kiss, and would explore with their mouth, fingers, and genitals all the openings, appendages, and pleasurable parts of each others' bodies. The sexual organs, mouth, rectum, and fingertips have the greatest numbers of nerve endings -- why? For an evolutionary, species-specific purpose.

I think there is an evolutionary development upward from mere reproductive-sex. As you ascend the scale of evolution play becomes more prevalent and frequent as an expression of the species life-force. Play appears to be important in the individual's brain development and creativity. Sexual play and its creative manifestations definitely seem to be correlated with education, intelligence, and creativity.

Allow your mind to roam freely. If recreational sex is an evolutionary step forward then what are the consequences? As with dolphins and apes the focus of the sex drive can be the opposite sex, the same sex, or a serial procedure in a group. Some dominant chimps have sex with one female after another. This binds them to him and he protects their offspring. In humans there could also be a bonding between each person as he/she gives pleasure to one or more others. People could indulge themselves in any temporary or permanent arrangements which brought them sexual pleasure. People like those who give them pleasure so this would be a larger, a stronger bonding then mere friendship without sex. The sexual pleasure would keep alive these bonds. Maybe that's one of its purposes.

Negatively, these arrangements could cause unwanted pregnancies and rampant disease. The first could be dealt with in many ways. Safe and effective contraceptive methods are available and in an adult, consensual environment, those involved would cooperate to avoid pregnancies and would do whatever was necessary if a pregnancy did occur. The more pressing problem of disease would also be more easily handled if recreational sex was socially accepted. A person would have regular medical check-ups and each person would be expected to be responsible. If one wasn't and others became ill, the offending party could be sued or jailed.

The main problem is that recreational sex, sex for personal pleasure, is viewed as immoral. Even in marriage until recently, a woman wasn't supposed to enjoy sex, but to endure it. Because of unwanted pregnancies and children who had to be supported by the community rather than the parents and the problem of disease, societies created strong taboos against recreational sex, especially for women. Men have always had greater license because they didn't bear children and they had greater power over their lives. There were good reasons against recreational sex which protected the health and welfare of the general population. These would no longer exist if society wasn't trapped in religious/cultural lags which are anachronisms.

The problem with recreational sex between consenting adults is that, like alcohol, those too young to act responsible also feel they should be allowed to indulge in the imitation of the adults. In many primitive communities, the young are allowed great sexual freedom. However, what works in one setting often does not in another. Therefore, I am not advocating recreational sex in a complex society until the person has passed the social hurdles necessary for financial independence or responsibility.

"Relief" sex: This is based on the idea, possibly mythological, that the sexual organs, especially in the male, build up physical tension which must be released. Wet dreams and more frequent masturbation by men and boys are used as proof. Some women say they have the same problem of needing sexual release or they get anxious and upset.

I do believe that each individual has his own rhythms of sexual need. These are affected by many internal factors such as exercise, sleep, nutritional patterns, and hormonal levels as well as externals such as job stress, social and financial responsibilities, and belief systems. These rhythms are as insistent to many as hunger is to all.

When I was a probation counselor in a juvenile hall, my section was filthy when I took over. I embarrassed the boys by telling them to take toilet paper with them to their rooms and place their ejaculations in the paper rather then on the ceilings and walls. Within one week I had the cleanest section with the calmest, most friendly boys in the hall.

We need to make ourselves more comfortable with our sexual rhythms and make masturbation an acceptable practice so children and adults can indulge their rhythms on an as-needed basis without guilt. Those who I have helped do so, children and adults, state they have been happier and can better relate to the opposite sex.

It is possible that some people have greater needs for sex in terms of frequency and time involved during the act just as there are differences in frequency and quantity of food eaten. Those with greater drives understand; those with smaller drives have difficulty appreciating the intensity of the need for relief-sex for some.

Relief sex can be a problem if the person feels guilty about masturbating, has no normal sexual outlets, or is married to a person who has very different needs and rhythms which don't coincide.

For relief sex you can masturbate, visit a prostitute, or use any consenting adult who is willing to meet your needs. If the consenting adult's your spouse and she gives in just to meet your needs, then she is engaging in duty sex which is an expression of her diminished self -- and yours. Although many would disagree, I would rather see you engaging in recreation sex with another consenting adult who selected you too and is in synch with your rhythms.

I don't believe relief sex, except masturbation or nocturnal emissions, expresses your giant self. I don't believe people using each other enhances either. In recreational sex, they are together by choice, know the limits of their relationships, give mutual pleasure, and show a mature responsibility to the relationship. They don't use another as is the case with relief sex.

Platonic nonsex. If two people get together in a romantic relationship without sex, I think they are in the wrong century. More than likely they are both teasers who don't have the genitals for a full-blooded relationship and are playing at both sex and love. They are either diminished by family or religious beliefs which prevent them from being honest and real.

I do think it is very possible for a man and woman to have a loving friendship without sex. I think they should be able to honestly discuss why sex will not be involved, but once the air is cleared, they could have a vital and fulfilling friendship. It isn't easy because in our society seeing a man and woman together a lot usually leads people to believe they have a sexual relationship (unless they're married which gives them the license, but sometimes neither wants to drive).

Thirty-Three

Love-Sex: Marriage

Love sex. If you agree that reproductive sex, relief sex, and recreational sex are progressions in an evolution of our species, then love sex is the latest development. Again, I do not equate love sex with the romantic, platonic, knight in shining armor and fair maiden of the Middle Ages. In that tradition the woman was treated as a beautiful thing to be worshipped, not possessed. The Victorian notion of a woman was a helpmate, but not a full-bodied sex partner. The romantic notions of early Hollywood treated women as things to be worshipped or possessed, but women were seldom seen as equals.

My belief is that men and women are of the same species, but are physiologically so different that it is very difficult for one sex to truly understand and appreciate how the other feels or sees the world. In fact, the world is experienced differently depending on your sex.

In love sex there is the attraction phase. This is usually biochemical. It also depends on the socialization of each as to what is deemed sexually desirable. Certain members of each sex are more attractive to greater numbers of the opposite sex. This is determined by cultural factors. Certain Polynesian cultures viewed large women who we see as overweight as extremely beautiful. Some find straight hair attractive, some like natural blondes, and so on.

There are people who believe each relationship is the result of previous karmic relationships which have specific learnings for each person. The attraction is the means for them to find each other. As a poet I like this idea, but as a scientist I tend to emphasize the biochemical/social.

Whatever the reasons for the attraction they are not as relevant as what they do with it. At this point there is no difference between love sex and the other types. What makes love sex so different?

I do not consider any relationship a love sex one until it has stood the test of time. Many people can manage to meet their own and another person's needs for weeks or months, even a few years. But to do this for years and decades, for each to create a giant self, endure life's trials and still want to be together, that sounds like love sex.

172

In most sexual relationships there is a large element of thingifying. One or both uses the other for his own pleasures, which is acceptable in recreation sex, but not in love sex. In love sex each is healthy enough to want, ask, or demand that his needs be met, but is equally concerned about the needs of his partner. This is an area of great differences. Man's biological rhythms, from his early evolution, were directed towards a fast erection without the need for much stimulation with an equally quick ejaculation. A quick response meant more efficient reproductive sex. Now, with women rightfully demanding that their unique biological rhythms be met also, more complex initial stimulation is required, more affection during love-making, delay in orgasm, and more talking afterwards.

This means constant adjustments and fine tuning from both so that the pendulum doesn't swing the other way and men are thingified. I remember during the early civil rights days, many of my Black friends wanted more than equality, they wanted revenge. Women have to be careful that they don't take their new powers and abuse them. If either party is used, it isn't love sex. Few people have achieved this balance because it is so difficult, but it is an evolutionary step upwards and more people will make the ascent.

Love sex is poetic, mysterious, and metaphoric. The generative and transformative character of love means that neither person remains the same. Each is transformed by the passion and caring of the other and is able to transcend his/her personal pettiness. These changes must enhance each person as he/she further develops more and more of her/his total human potentials. Since each develops his abilities at different rates jealousy, unavoidable rejection, and misunderstanding will occur and must be met with patience and maturity. This is why it is critical for both to be independent enough to mentally and emotionally stand on his/her own. This minimizes the feelings of rejection when the other needs to be alone, as is sometimes necessary for personal growth. Dependent people cannot tolerate this need of occasional solitude and it destroys their relationships.

I do not mean that each person must be totally financially, mentally, and emotionally independent before he can have a love sex relation. No one is ever totally independent and one of the purposes of the relationship is that together each can realize this potentials more easily.

Love sex is a fusion of two disparate entities, each able to retain its own identity, yet together create a third entity which includes both. The pleasure and passions of sex are the heated crucible in which they combine their separate elements into an alloy reflecting the best of both. They add and multiply their mental, emotional, physical, and spiritual selves into an entity stronger than any other earthly relationship.

Love-sex should be stronger than blood ties because parents and children bring a social/biological obligation into play. True love sex is always a relationship of choice. Your parents will always be your parents, your children will remain your children, but you and your love-sex partner have to keep the relationship alive by what you continually create together. It is the acceptance of the uncertainty and insecurity of any human relationship which keeps the love sex bond the most meaningful of relationships. There is commitment to the other, but not to the extent that it smothers or blocks the other's growth.

To often one person in the relationship, acting from his diminished self, pressures the other to do, feel, or act in ways that also limit or diminish her. You should be aware when you are acting from a position of fear. If you are afraid to be yourself with your partner, you have not achieved a love sex relationship. In this relationship each party is searching to be his giant self, preferably within the context of the relationship, but not afraid to be himself in other secondary contexts. You should be able to learn from, spend time with, and enjoy the company of one or more people of either sex without feeling you are diminishing the love sex partner.

These other relationships are necessary because no one person can meet another's total needs. Others should be able to meet these needs without the partner feeling jealous or diminished. Other relationships bring knowledge and experiences back to the primary love sex partnership and enrich and enliven it.

In the beginning love sex is not blind, but it functions on levels of non-ordinary reality. Its powers enable the lovers to be in a different reality, which is why they look so silly to others. Their actions are freer, more spontaneous, less constrained by convention because the rest of the world is not very important. As time progresses it becomes more difficult to sustain these levels of passion and social isolation. This is where most couples fail. They cannot sustain their own intimacy as the social world gradually intrudes. In love sex the pair manages to grow together while moving back and forth between their relationship and other social realities.

It is not easy and there are few guidelines because true love sex partners are blazing new paths, a new type of human relationship.

Frankly, I know of no couple which has totally managed to do this, but I'd like to meet those who think they have. I see it as an ideal, (as being a Christian is a religious ideal which few attain) a goal to work towards, rather than an established fact. This new kind of partnership would mean that two individuals who were basically healthy in all ways and who were strong enough to be independent chose to be interdependent. It would mean two giant selves meeting and selecting to remain with each other for even greater growth.

Marie and I have maintained a level of passion and growth longer than most, but neither of us has successfully coped with some of his/her demons from the past. (Unfinished business haunts and cripples most attempts to move to the level of love sex.) We have been learning from our mistakes, but our giant selves are under constant attack by our diminished selves.

What has marriage to offer to those who would like to work towards a love sex relationship?

Well first: Social approval. You may say, "Who cares?" The truth is that everyone cares. Almost without exception humans need others as much when they are grown as they did as dependent children. When I speak about each person being independent in an ideal relationship, I do not mean it in any absolute sense. I mean the degree to which each can allow the other to follow his needs and to develop his abilities alone as well as together for growth, comfort, security, and love.

The two people cannot live in isolation without others any more than either can fully develop his giant self without the other. The more interdependent the couple becomes the more they will need and be able to take from others too. The time wasted playing power games, the tiring behaviors resulting from petty fears and jealousies, and the constant attention-getting ploys which are the daily fare in most marriages are minimized in a love sex one. This frees both to be more fully involved with one another when that is what they both choose, to be alone, or to be elsewhere with other people.

The intelligent couple is mature and secure enough to move freely through society without the possessiveness and jealousy which cripples most relationships. This does not mean each "doing his own thing" without concern about the other. It means the opposite. There is a constant level of concern which results in continuous openness, communication, and compromises both can live with.

Love sex begins with mutual attraction, respect, and concern. It grows and flowers into a relationship in which each is a helpmate for the other in creating and expanding his/her giant self to its highest levels.

This can rarely occur in isolation and needs a social context. Since they need others, social contexts, the couple needs the approval only society can give. Therefore, marriage appears to be an essential part of love sex.

However, since I do believe time together is an essential criterion of love-sex, social approval should not be given until a minimum of ten years has been spent together. A special license or certificate could be given by the state which would give them tax and other benefits because these people would be the most socially responsible. Then the license must be renewed every ten years or they become legally and automatically divorced. This acceptance of the uncertainty of life should help those who need marriage as they ascend the evolutionary ladder and will be of no concern to those who don't.

Couples can enter marriage for relief sex, recreation sex, or reproductive sex. Most will enter for a combination of reasons and they should receive social approval. I don't think anyone should enter marriage with the idea that it is temporary. However, the maturity levels at the time, the intensity of the sexual attraction, the levels of dependency-interdependency, the unfinished business from parents and other relationships, and the realities of daily living cause most marriages to fail.

Living together is an answer for some. Possibly marriages should begin with a five year contract which could be renewed or dissolved with everything settled ahead of time like a pre-nuptial agreement. This proposal takes away the romance, but places the relationship on a more realistic basis. Since in our society the government is expected to help pick up the pieces of disturbed or destroyed relationships, it should have a say in how they are entered into and dissolved. Therefore, there should be heavy financial penalties (taxes) for any couple having children with the first contract. Once they have proven they can be responsible, not a burden to society, then they should be allowed to have children without tax penalties.

I know this sounds dictatorial and seems to be against much of what I've said about the development of individual rights and responsibilities. However, I have spent a lifetime in public schools and working with juvenile authorities. I have seen the effects of parents who were still children trying to raise children. They created unloved and unloving people and perpetuated poverty.

I would not give welfare to any unmarried teenager. I have taught sex education for years. Most girls get pregnant to get out of their homes, to get out of school, to have someone who they believe will be dependent upon them, and who will love them. The boys want to get girls pregnant because they see it as an indication of their manhood, plus for some of the same reasons the girls give.

As I said earlier, no one can have total freedom if he elects to be part of a society. These children and their parents demand to be taken care of even when they make irresponsible choices. There is no way we can keep them from having relief or recreation sex, but we can say no to reproductive sex for those who cannot be financially responsible.

For an unmarried teenager or any woman without the ability to support her child, abortion should be mandatory. If she and her parents, her boy friend, and her religious leaders demand she have the right to have the child, then they should all sign the legal documents to assure that the government will have no obligation in caring for the child. And, the government should not be blackmailed into paying for the child.

I realize that this seems to make me an enemy of the poor, but the opposite is true. I took the responsibility of a yours, mine, and ours relationship. Even with a good job and always a second, I couldn't make ends meet and went bankrupt once. I know how difficult it is to give your children what they need, but I took it on because I was financially able to do so. I see how frustrated and angry poor parents are. I see how angry and frustrated their children are. Most do not have healthy relationships. Of course, you can always point out exceptions in which the parents or the children or both flourished despite poverty. But they are just that, exceptions.

Marriages fail, relationships fail because the couples do not have the skills of developing good relationships. If babies raise babies they never learn these skills and thereby perpetuate poor parenting and make poor candidates for marriage. Society then carries the burden in welfare and crime. I'm proud of being a liberal and a person who has spent a lifetime championing the causes of the underdog. I think that what I propose will help end the vicious cycle of poverty which is the result of racism and sexism.

In my school program I do everything possible to help my students realize the forces which diminish them and what they can do to develop their giant selves. They return each day to environments which undermine and kill almost everything I do. Despite it, an impact is made upon most of them and many are escaping the cycle. But it is obvious that their belief that they can do whatever they want with their bodies and someone else will take the responsibility is totally supported by our churches and government.

I would not want us to be so callous to human suffering that we let people die in the streets as they do in so many parts of the world. However, as long as we support irresponsibility, it will flourish. And if the state is expected to pick up the tab then it has the right to determine specific conditions.

By society setting up the appropriate conditions for responsibility in sex and human relations at the most primitive, biological levels, the couples will learn what is necessary for more and more people to achieve higher levels of human functioning. As it stands now the rich get richer at the expense of the poor. The poor do not realize that their belief systems are what keep them poor. Irresponsibility for their sexual drives keeps them as breeders for cheap labor. The rich who pay little in taxes but are responsible for the laws which seem Christian and generous, profit from this irresponsibility. So do the churches who promise a better life while perpetuating poverty and ignorance.

Couples need the sanction, the social approval of their society. Marriage is the social/legal means that society has of creating the best conditions for a couple and (if they wish and are able to support them) their children.

At this time, in distortion of freedom and the right for anyone to give birth, we have supported a belief system which allows and perpetuates irresponsibility for one's actions. Our laws need to be changed to make divorce easier and entering marriage more difficult, and finally making the right to have children the most difficult. This can only occur when the government stops making poverty seem profitable. To the poor the little they get seems like a lot, but it is this illusion which keeps them poor.

Stricter laws and social values regarding marriage and having children will not just save money, it will enable more and more people to enter the kind of long-lasting relationships which will encourage the creation of their giant selves.

The love sex lifetime bonding is an ideal which more couples could attempt until the ideal would become reality.

Thirty-Four

Mistakes As Learning Opportunities

Although I said that laws need to be passed to make marriage and having children more difficult and divorce easier, I believe firmly that human mistakes are unavoidable. We should use them as learning opportunities. This does not mean we should not take every kind of precaution and think ahead to avoid mistakes. However, they do occur and we need to rethink their value.

Mistakes are seen as indications of something lacking in the person who made the error. It is felt by the person that the error is a reflection of a permanent lack or an irreversible condition within him.

Example: A child spills milk and is called stupid. He cannot tie his shoes correctly so he is called stupid. He doesn't bring his dad his beer quickly enough -- stupid. Every time he makes any kind of error, he is stupid. He has developed a conditioned response towards errors. An error equals stupidity -- his. Since everyone makes all kinds of errors daily, he is constantly reminded of his stupidity. No one can live this way without some reaction. Most people react by enjoying the errors of others and jumping in to point out their stupidity. By turning the spotlight on someone else their pains are temporarily eased. Always someone is feeling diminished as a person.

Placing a real value on learning from mistakes changes the entire picture. Example: I teach spelling by giving the children words they've seldom seen or been asked to spell. They are used to getting a list and studying it. I just say a word and ask them to spell it. At first many are angry and scared. I explain that spelling is very complex and even easy words don't often look like they're spelled. But by having fun and trying a lot of unfamiliar words every day they'll be better spellers. I give the word, give them time to try and spell it, show them that many of their errors are very sensible, but that there is one arbitrary way that is considered correct. After awhile they lose their fear of spelling. Their writing, spelling, and reading improves but more importantly I've taught them to value and to learn from their errors.

I let even first graders correct most of their own papers. In all the grades they giggle and think they're putting one over on me -- legalized cheating. Some do abuse this privilege, but most become aware that I do this because I believe they will learn much more by becoming aware of their mistakes if they find them rather than if I do. I seldom comment on their errors unless I think they have not been trying, they're cheating, or I have noticed some pattern which helps me understand why they made the errors.

I do the same thing with students' behavior problems. I seldom lecture the class as a whole. When a student is in trouble, my thrust is for him to understand and accept responsibility for it. There are some things which have consequences which have been decided upon in advance by the class and by me. Once the misbehaving child has been heard and he acknowledges his error, then (if necessary, because sometimes his awareness is all he needs to avoid repeating the act) we decide the consequences together. In this way, he is not diminished by his negative behavior, but it is used to help him profit from it.

With our children, Marie and I applied the same belief system. When Eric was caught stealing we spent quite a bit of time first getting him to admit that he'd been doing so for months. Next, we discussed appropriate consequences. At no time was a decision imposed upon him, but rather he was involved in using his mistake to change his behavior. He is an adult and claims he never stole again.

When my dad caught me stealing he spanked me and threw into the furnace a very expensive sailboat which I loved. I was lectured at, yelled at, and spanked. He thought he had done the right thing by diminishing me, because he never again had to deal with my stealing. What happened was I was never careless again. I and the gang I created stole hundreds of dollars of items, sneaked into theaters, and vandalized for years without anyone getting caught. I did learn from my original mistake; I learned to be the king of thieves. I also learned about overkill which I have tried to avoid as an adult.

We can learn from our mistakes but we don't always learn from them at the time we should or could. With my ex-wife every time she refused to have sex with me I felt rejected, then angry. My immaturity and hers in this area were a part of our failure as a couple. The same thing began to happen with Marie. This was partly unfinished business with my ex and other women and partly from my inability to be honest about my feelings. By telling Marie that I was hurt first, then angry, she was able to realize that my rejection and anger towards her stemmed from my fears. Her refusal seemed to me to mean that I was not sexually satisfying or attractive to her. Most of the time Marie encouraged my giant self, but at these times I felt insignificant, diminished.

Gradually, I saw her as a unique person with a different sexual rhythm than mine. It didn't always coincide with mine and at those times she didn't feel like making love. I was finally able to see this not as a put-down of myself, but as an assertion of her right to express her needs. Seen this way I was still left with the problem but not anything diminishing to me.

Pain is another determiner of something gone wrong. If it is seen as a physical indicator, then you can use it to figure out the cause and then the cure. For years I suffered from headaches. My mother had them too so we took aspirin and suffered through them. When I became an athlete I had them less frequently and intensely. When we moved from the Midwest to California I was able to get outside more and exercise. I still had headaches and I learned about psychology so I assumed I was neurotic. It was much later in life that I discovered that my headaches mainly came from the amount of chocolate I ate daily and the kind of exercise I had. I suffered needlessly for years because I did not learn from my pain. Now I use my physical pains as my body's way to inform me of what I need to change.

Even knowing and believing what I do about mistakes, I must admit when I make them (especially ones caused by inattention) I feel stupid. Most of the time I try to laugh at myself (before others do) and then forgive myself. When I used to get lost because I'd misread a map or had not fully understood the directions, I'd get furious and (of course) blame my wife, the maps, the city, but never myself. I seldom would go into a service station -- too degrading. Now, as soon as I realize I'm lost, I pull into a service station (with several language translators in the trunk). I still get angry with myself because I haven't prepared properly, but it doesn't last long, much to Marie's relief.

All through the book I have been trying to get you to recognize how institutions and people make you function from your diminished self. My explaining all the ways you can make errors was not to put you down, but to get you to change your attitude about errors. If you are to create your giant self, you must accept your own and others' errors, and then use them as learning opportunities. (Read this to your boss, parent, teacher, or spouse.)

Thirty-Five

Guilt Can Be Useful

Guilt is useful? How can I say that? Almost the entire edifice of modern psychiatry has been built upon eradicating guilt. I feel that psychiatry has failed to recognize guilt when it is a productive message, a way of recognizing a mistake, pain, and a logical consequence for a person who has done something to hurt another.

I know that people and institutions purposely make you feel guilty in order to control your behavior even if the induced guilt is damaging to you. This type of guilt needs to be eradicated and I hope this book helps. When you are made to feel guilty by your mother because she is compulsive and has a fit each time you drop a crumb on the floor, that is irrational guilt. When your teacher makes you feel guilty because you go to the toilet too often, he is also irrationally imposing his standards upon you. These are abuses of guilt. Whenever guilt is used to control you because of the power-seeking motives or neurosis of the other, then it is an abuse of guilt.

When I spoke to delinquent youths I watched them to see whether or not they felt guilty. A sense of guilt and remorse, an awareness of how their actions had hurt others, was a reasonable barometer of their ability to be rehabilitated. They knew this and tried to fake guilt and remorse. In fact, the concept of rehabilitation is connected with creating in the criminal an awareness of the effects of his crime as well as the reasons for it. The development of a conscience in a child is society's mechanism to teach him to share and be considerate of others. Guilt is the feedback, the trained self-inflicted punishment to let him know he's done wrong.

If I hadn't provided for my children when I had the means to do so, I should have felt guilty. If I degrade or insult Marie, children, or anyone who has not harmed me, then I should feel guilty. If I do a shabby job, I should feel guilty.

Guilt is a bodily experience. It is a form of physical pain. It is good because it measures how badly I feel. I suffer minor discomfort when I forget to call my mother once a week. I suffer great pain when I purposely hurt anyone I love. And, I should.

Since the pain of the guilt is felt in my body I have the ability to control and relieve this pain. I can do so by somehow making it up to the person I've hurt. If the pain of guilt had not existed I might not have been aware of the pain I caused the other person. Her pain becomes mine. In the process I learn what I need to do to end our pain. Absence of pain is one way of knowing the situation has been resolved.

When you feel guilty, examine the reasons for it. If you have done something wrong whether it was done inadvertently or purposefully, admit it. Rectify it by making it up to the other in a way which satisfies him or her.

Often when you feel guilty you deny it and blame the victim. Throughout history man has always cleverly blamed his victim and often the victim accepted it. As a young psychologist I bought the nonsense about the rapist being seduced by his victim. I knew women were seductive and I was confused by my own fears and feelings. I wanted women and blamed them for allegedly making me want them. I blamed them for getting raped.

Now I find the idea ludicrous. These women were victims of some man's need to overpower women. It had little to do with sex, but a lot to do with powerlessness. The women did not want to be degraded, physically abused, or killed. The women did not have to do anything to provoke the rape, because the problem came entirely from within the rapist. The women were objects, things for him to work through his anger on.

Rape is an example of how we distort reality so we don't have to face the responsibility for our actions. Man can and does rationalize any or all of his behaviors, but if he has a conscience, that nagging reality in his body, that felt sense of personal responsibility will surface as guilt.

How do you evaluate whether or not you should feel guilty? After all, I've shown how certain people and institutions purposely make you feel guilty merely to control you for their uses, not for your own good, but theirs. How do you know when you're being used or should feel guilty?

It's not always easy. Making others feel guilty is learned very early in life. It's a powerful weapon, especially if the other person cares for or loves you. And everyone tries to get you to do what he or she wants.

Examine the situation. What is the other getting from it? What are you? What is he asking you to do? Why is he asking you? Could someone else do it? Did he ask someone else? Why or why not? What are the consequences if you don't meet his needs? What are your responsibilities to him? What do you want to do?

What should you do if you have wronged a person? Allow yourself to feel his and your pain, your guilt. Ask yourself what the feeling is telling you. Look at your relationship with him and see if your guilt is justified. What part is rational, what is illogical? What is emotional and based on feelings you may have trouble justifying to others? Listen to the wronged party because he might have a perspective you don't. Sometimes a friend or relative can help you get your perspective so you can sort out your feelings and use your guilt properly.

Treat it like a temporary illness. Would the medication which is making up with the injured party be good for you? You need to take a hard look at yourself and your behavior. What can or are you willing to do? What can that person realistically expect from you from now on? What is she/he willing to do to make things better?

Let your guilt be useful indicator of the problem. Find out what each is willing to do to resolve the problem. Change what you can, accept and live with the rest because you can't let guilt pervade your life. Benefit from its uses, but don't let it cripple you.

Thirty-Six

Laughter: The Aha! Of Ha-Ha!

Without laughter there can be not giant self. Laughter enables you to see yourself and the world in a more livable perspective. There are times when you need to see things crazily, non-seriously. If you didn't and everything was deadly serious you would become totally pessimistic. Laughter causes healthy physiological and psychological changes in your body/mind. So as you need a coffee break as an interlude in your routine, a way to clear your head and rejuvenate you body, you need laughter breaks throughout the day. A laughter break is fun and is good for you.

Dr. Fry, a Stanford researcher, has proven many of laaaauuuughter's (doesn't that spelling tickle you?) beneficial effects. Norman Cousins' miraculous cure of what had been diagnosed as a terminal illness and years later, his remarkable recovery from a heart attack, are attributed to his prescribing laughter for himself.

Endorphins, those wonderful morphine-like drugs that your brain releases, are activated by laughter. Drug addicts, think of the money you'd save by laughing rather than popping, though laughter is also very addicting. It isn't your imagination, it's the drug your body has manufactured being released into your blood stream which makes you feel so good when you laugh. Since you feel good you have a more positive attitude towards life and other people. Laughing makes you happy.

One of the many reasons I love Marie is she usually laughs at my puns and straight-faced remarks. We are fairly youthful looking, but both of us have some heavy-duty laugh wrinkles. A heavy cosmetic price to pay, but with all the kids we raised on a limited budget it was laughter or tears. Laughter is good for the digestion, which is why we are a family of eager-eaters.

We even yakked it up at breakfast, which was an effort for some of the clan. By dinner everyone was ready and needed to laugh a lot. Eric and my ex-son-in-law, Mark, are the only bona fide story-tellers, but everyone used to tell something horrendous that happened which we could defuse with laughter.

We have laughed at teachers, supervisors, bosses, subordinates, peers, and occasionally at me. We laughed as we heard how these people mishandled things or hurt our feelings. In the process besides the catharsis, the relief, we often found better ways to handle the people or the situation. After the laughter has died one of us saw things from a different, a fresh perspective, and was able to communicate it to the diminished person. The victim then had a certain empathy and understanding for the victimizer and could more effectively deal with him.

Without a sense of humor, without laughter, all the things I've told you about unavoidable errors and how your institutions diminish you, would be terribly grim. All your errors would make you suicidal or homicidal or genocidal, or the worst one of all authoricidal!

There are jokes that are sick and offensive to various people and the butts of these jokes are rightfully offended and angry. However, even these jokes, if they could be taken lightly instead of personally, would often clear the air. By bursting through our pomposity we usually don't destroy human dignity, but place it in a more human perspective. Many times, with minority friends, we have unmercifully teased one another about our racial or ethnic backgrounds. There is an element of hostility because we are all prejudiced to varying degrees, but knowing the other person cares allows us to ventilate without anger.

The more realistically you see yourself, the closer you get to going beyond the boundaries of your normal humanity. Your giant self should be able to enjoy a giant guffaw, even if it is at your own expense. Many times I have defused tense classroom situations by humor. Although, in recalling them, I am not clear if they were laughing with me or at me. (Oh, well...)

Another reason I love Marie is that she can laugh at herself almost as hard as she laughs at me. Many times when one of us has been ready to go out the door, to a bar, or somewhere to escape the other, one manages to see how ridiculous she or he is acting and makes a comment which makes the other laugh. It doesn't always happen so easily, but laughter is one of our main tools to maintain balance in our lives.

I believe if you aren't laughing at yourself, there's probably lots and lots of people who are. I'd rather laugh with them. Today during a moment when the class was noisy I angrily said, "Give me a hand!" instead of "Raise your hand." One girl smiled and clapped. Despite my anger, I bowed, smiled, and called on a child with his hand up. Laughter kept me from acting more stupidly. Without this ability to see yourself in a humorous vein, your giant self can never be more than a dwarf.

How do you develop your sense of humor if it is presently lacking? Here's a sure-fire method. Start by looking at yourself in the mirror. If you can't find anything funny, you're probably kidding yourself or looking at someone else by mistake. Listen, as cute as I am, I am funny-looking too. I mean the two sides of my face (and yours too), hey, they don't match. We're all lop-sided, lop-eared, and lop-nosed.

Didn't work for you? Still not laughing at yourself? Then take off all your clothes and stand in front of a full-length mirror. Imagine you had a large audience. All those people laughing would cause such vibrations that the building would collapse. Still sober-faced? You're really impressed with yourself aren't you? Try this. Turn around with your behind facing the mirror. You're still naked. Bend down, look between your legs, peek at yourself, and smile. If you're pompous even from that perspective, your a pompous ass!

Forgive me for being vulgar (which means common), but if you are to cope with your fears and expand your giant self, you need to face reality as well as learn to recognize your potentials. A sense of humor is a critical mechanism to keep you balanced. You should be able to see (and accept) yourself as you are which is ludicrous, ridiculous, animal-like as well as what you could be, your giant self and god-like.

I've always been disturbed while teaching social studies to children because the people in illustrated text books never have sex (but have babies), never go to the toilet (but smile a lot anyway), and never do any of the obnoxious and disgusting things that all of us do because our bodies make sounds, have odors, and do things which we wish they'd do more quietly. As with your picture in the mirror, denying these things doesn't make them go away, it makes them more difficult to handle.

If the mirror picture was dealt with easily by you, then aging probably will be too. As you age you lose your powers, your looks, and you become more dependent upon others. Ultimately, if you live long enough, you'll be as helpless as a baby. At that point you may have to be fed, bathed, and taken to the toilet. Despite my glibness, I find this embarrassing. Unless I conquer this my hospital stay or my aging will become a monstrous problem. If I accept my body and its functions as natural, then I will have fewer problems in the end (accidental pun).

I am not suggesting you guffaw your way through life and take nothing seriously or sacred. I don't let the children in my classes tease each other (I try to minimize it, because it goes on despite my efforts), because they don't have the maturity or training to keep from fighting. They would be happier and healthier if they could take their differences less seriously and defensively. Jokes can defuse rather than incite, but not when one party is totally operating from his diminished self. Fanatics (diminished selves who burlesque being human beings) have no sense of humor and consequently show little common sense.

Morons, people with damaged brains and limited intellectual abilities, smile and laugh at everything. This is not our kind of laughter because they do not understand humor, but rather it reflects the goodness of their nature. So, I'm not suggesting you act like a moron and smile continuously, but use humor as a balance to the unpleasantness and unhappiness that are part of the human condition. Laugh to keep your balance and retain your sense of what is important and valuable in life.

In your relationships consciously try to see the ridiculous, the pompous, and the limiting in people and events. You not only get the feeling of relief, the healthy physical-emotional relief of laughter, but you will be surprised as you find new solutions to old problems. Your laughter and humor enables you to see everyone and everything in different ways. This is the essence of creative problem-solving. This fresh view may be your opening towards a clearer vision, a compromise that will satisfy you and the others involved.

Example: Visualize the person you most dislike. Take off his clothes and dress him ridiculously. Next time you see him be careful because you'll see him that way. By laughing at him, you'll feel more comfortable (this is not a giant self activity) and be able to handle him if he's always putting you down.

From this kind of laughter you should be able to ascend the scale of humor and go from pie-in-the-face to cosmic humor. If you bought that cosmic humor bit, then you've just gotten egg on your face. These experiences should give you an Aqua Velva insight into the Aha of Ha Ha -- and make you feel better.

Thirty-Seven

Care of Your Body

I am not going to belabor this chapter because there are thousands of excellent articles and hundreds of books written by experts in health care. My doctorate in nutrition makes me expert enough to say you need to read magazines like SELF-CARE and AMERICAN HEALTH to keep up with the increased new knowledge available.

The mind/body connection for good health has been firmly established and this book emphasizes the role of your consciousness in creating a healthy mind which can create an equally healthy body.

We know exercise is important and it can be adjusted to your schedule, age, and athleticism. I've had to give up some of the more vigorous spots like touch football or racquetball because of knee and back problems. I get plenty of exercise by twenty minutes of rowing or cycling at least four times a week.

Sleep can range from almost none to twelve hours a day. The important thing is that you must know your body/mind well enough to determine what is best for you. You should also be flexible enough to compensate for the times your needs vary.

There is presently a small war between the dieticians and nutritionists for the minds and bodies of America. Dieticians come from a background more closely tied to medical doctors and hospitals. They tend to believe in nutrition allied to a medical model of a sick body which needs to be cured by medication. This is a free-wheeling generalization. Not all dieticians believe this.

Nutritionists are more often allied with non-traditional healers such as chiropractors, homeopathic physicians, and even practitioners of native and folk medicine. Their emphasis is more on prevention of illness, encouragement of good health habits, and the liberal use of vitamins and minerals prescribed on an individual basis. Since many of their techniques and remedies are not acceptable to doctors, they are not as acceptable to the general public as the dieticians are.

When I was studying for my doctorate in nutrition many of the ideas I was learning about were being damned in some of the traditional medical journals I read. Now, several yours later, the same things which were attacked are being extolled as proper medical routines or useful supplements.

I would not place my total trust in a non-traditional practioner anymore than I would in a board certified doctor. The message of SELF-CARE magazine is that your health should be in your own hands. Doctors are experts in disease, but few are well versed in good health. Most are themselves over-stressed, unbalances between their physical, mental, social, sexual, emotional, and spiritual selves.

My message has been (and is) that you need to listen to your body and learn its mysterious and wondrous rhythms. You can train, even force it to obey rhythms which you impose upon it. Sometimes this works, but more often, your body either sabotages your carefully constructed plans for it or it makes you ill, even killing those who constantly ignore it. I've explained who, what, and how this was done to you. If you want to maximize your health and create your giant self, you need to learn about you body.

This means having some idea of how the body actually functions. But, most importantly, it means destroying the conception that anyone knows your body better than you do. You have to wrest your body from your doctors and regain what you gave up to your parents, schools, work, and society and discover what your rhythms are. Once you know them, it is a lifetime task to refine this knowledge, you will know how much to sleep, what and how much to eat, and how to regulate your exercise plans.

Everyone says that he is to busy to do all the things he knows he should do for his body because his job, family, or something will suffer. Nonsense! It's a question of values, a change in perspective. For years I heard teachers tell me that they admired me because I gave my children art, music, and physical education almost every day. They could have done it, but they didn't value these subjects. I knew these activities helped the children become better students because they stimulated the brain differently than the usual academics did. So, during every year I had the happiest, most well-rounded children. During testing, they did as well or better than comparable classes.

You need to make the decision that whatever caused you to lose contact with your body rhythms can be reversed. You can learn to listen to your body rhythms and respond appropriately to them. By listening to your body, learning and responding to its rhythms, you will be able to restructure your life to maximize your physical health and well-being. By doing this you will have the basic physical structure to create your giant self.

Thirty-Eight

Forgiveness, A Divine Experience

I would rewrite the saying "To err is human; to forgive, divine," to this : To err is a constant human experience, to forgive is downright incredible. Forgiving may not be impossible because some enlightened and evolutionarily developed souls do seem to forgive, but for most people forgiveness is beyond them. Why?

The brilliant brain with its tremendous storage capabilities retains everything. It stores data which has little or no emotional meaning to you. It is its nature to make sense out of everything or at least to organize and file it. Even if you can not understand data or an event as it really is (whatever that may mean), you force it into some pattern so it can be filed and stored according to a system you have created. When an experience has an emotional load, which means many other parts of the cortical brain merge with the limbic and reptilian brain as well as other body systems, you have unforgettable experiences. Load the brain up further with the strongest kinds of emotions functioning at peak levels in which pain, fear, anger, and hatred are blinding the usual social monitors, then you have experiences which are potentially unforgivable.

Your brain cannot forget anything or anyone which causes you emotional pain. Time makes such an experience less painful, but with slight cues you can recall the incident quickly. Its vividness depends on the number of cues, their intensity, and the recency of the event. These cues or triggers are frequently set off innocently by events or others than the one who injured you. Your brain then generalizes from familiar fragments and you unwittingly fill in the gory and inappropriate details. These moments keep the pain alive and even reinforce it.

Your personal myth and unfinished business play strange games with your reconstruction and memories of the past in ways by which the previous hurts are reinforced. And, you seldom are able to forgive hurts if you're convinced you were victimized. It is made worse if the person didn't apologize, admit he wronged you, and made no effort to correct the wrong.

Yet, even if you are able to overcome your natural resistances to forgiving, a nagging voice warns you. This is a healthy, protective device so you won't be abused again. It will not let you forget and hopefully keeps you from being hurt again by the same person, event, or one which you see as similar. It is wise to be careful, but look around you at all the people who avoid intimate, loving experiences because they have been or believe they have been wronged and hurt. They are letting their diminished selves rule their lives.

However, you can replace the negative with positive experiences with that person or group as you give them another opportunity. You should be cautious, but if enough positive and satisfying things occur, they may be able to counterbalance the negatives which you are trying to forget in the process of forgiving.

Unless you're an idiot, your brain keeps reminding you to beware of this fool so he doesn't continue victimizing you. It is a useful protective device. You are programmed towards mistrust and that's healthy in a world where people generally place their own self-interest before yours or often act at your expense. Jesus' belief in turning the other check is an evolutionary giant step which few humans can manage. It is an ideal and I don't think you should demand it of yourself.

Why bother to forgive? (You know you can't forget because the negative experience is embedded in your brain/body.) What's in it for you?

By forgiving you become more healthy emotionally, mentally, and make powerful strides spiritually. If you're working towards an effective, balanced giant self forgiveness is a necessity. But what your diminished self wants is vengeance; it doesn't want to forgive, it wants to get even. You would like god's powers of punishment to make your victimizers suffer the way you have. Perfectly normal, but completely unproductive. Forgiving is not just spiritually healthy, it has practical advantages.

When you forgive you feel an amazing sense of accomplishment. Both you and you opponent feel a weight lifted. This weight had been burdening both of you and not just in your mutual relationship. Through the process of generalizing your resentment has affected many others. By forgiving you begin to regain control over your own life. The anger and pain are lessened and you can enjoy your life more.

For many yours I blamed my ex-father-in-law because of his interference in my life. He was partly responsible for my divorce and had an even greater role in my not getting custody of my daughters. Time lessened my anger and when the girls became women I better understood (although I still didn't agree with) his interference. I wrote him a letter and told him how I appreciated what he had done for Robin because I believed he had helped her. I couldn't say that about Lisa because I felt he continued to harm her. Yet though he never mentioned the letter, there was a mutuality of respect shown to each other that had not previously been present. Before he died we had each completed much unfinished business. Our forgiving each other to the degree we could enabled me to be closer to my daughters and the rest of my ex-wife's family. My letter helped many more people that just him and myself. In this sense forgiveness is not just a personally redeeming act, it is an expression of your giant self. It is socially integrating. It is a healing as powerful as any medical cure.

As a maverick, a rebel in every adult job I ever had, I have always irritated those who were my legal superiors. In my twenties I didn't care what they thought or felt and I spent a lot of wasted effort battling windmills of my own creation. I would never apologize or forgive. As I got smarter I realized that by apologizing I took the wind out of my supervisors' sails and if they persisted in haranguing me they looked foolish. It was a psychological manipulation and I would watch their surprise and discomfort as they squirmed. After all, here I was admitting my errors, placing myself at their mercy, so how could they do anything but forgive? But they wanted revenge, they wanted to inflict pain in the name of changing my behavior. Yet I was saying I did wrong and wouldn't do it again. They were trapped and I loved watching them struggle with their power which I had turned around. I had created an art form against those who abused their power or were trying to control me.

As I matured I began to appreciate the dilemmas of the supervisors and I tried to understand how they saw their jobs and mine. When I apologized it was sincere because I realized how my behavior affected them. I saw them as partners, not as the enemy.

Example: A letter I planed to send to the local newspaper was intended to show how our school was successfully coping with integration, not just desegregation. I asked the school secretary to type it. She showed it to the principal who asked to see me. The principal said she couldn't allow the secretary to type the letter and she requested that I not send it. My old feelings welled up, but I calmed myself down and asked her why. She explained how she thought most people reading the letter would take it. I truly listened to her and was able to see what she saw. She was correct so I had the choice of rewriting the letter or destroying it. I thanked her and tore it up. I avoided a situation which would have made two friends into unnecessary enemies.

Many situations which could necessitate forgiveness are avoidable when people operate from their giant selves. Obviously it is easier to head off a problem than it is to correct it once it has blossomed.

Since one message in this book is the difficulty of avoiding human error, it means that whether you're the believed victim or the alleged victimizer, forgiveness is a chance for both of you to grow. In the above example the principal could have used her legal powers and forbidden me to write a letter about the school. I could have countered with my constitutional rights and we'd have been in a serious conflict. Mutual respect and concern were reflections of our giant selves.

Forgiveness is one of the highest characteristics of an emerging giant self. You must be able to forgive those who have hurt you, inadvertently or purposefully. And you must be able to forgive yourself, even if the other, acting from his diminished self, won't or is unable to do so.

During the time I was making peace with my ex-father-in-law, I was actively and consciously trying to mend all my broken emotional fences. I had been coming to grips with my mortality and didn't want to leave any unfinished business behind the way my father had. I seriously looked at all my relationships and tried to fix them. I forgave the others, myself, and wanted them to forgive me and themselves.

One close friend had drifted away for many reasons, some my fault, some his. I called, wrote, and we got together. Our families enjoyed the visit and I thought we were going to resume our friendship. It didn't happen. I didn't hear from him again. I realize the fallacy in making assumptions, but I believe I know why he didn't wish to rekindle our friendship. I may be wrong. In any event I did what I needed to do to forgive him and be forgiven. It is no longer my problem. I miss him and I will always love him because he has been a significant person in my life as I have been in his. We have much to offer one another so maybe, in the future, he will be able to shed his diminished self, forgive, and we will be able to be good friends.

To forgive is to enter a totally different ethical-moral framework. Forgiveness is not included with face-saving, competition, personal manipulation, eye for an eye mentality, or merely giving in to the wishes of others, or with any of the usual things which pass for morality. Unlike conditional love, forgiving can be done without reciprocity. It is more satisfying if the forgiver and forgiven share consciously in the experience. It also enables both to grow, whereas if it's one-sided, the forgiver is the sole beneficiary. You forgive because you wish to grow and to help others rise above their egos and animal-dominated natures into a spiritual realm. Forgiveness is a mode of growth similar to the intrinsic pleasure one gets from learning and creativity. It is its own reward. It can be taught. It ennobles you.

What if the person has hurt you, but doesn't believe or know he has done so? He will not believe he needs to apologize nor be forgiven.

Stanley Milgram's experiments seemed to prove that decent human beings all over the world would, if they were convinced the experimental subject was a bad person, give him electrical shocks to the point of killing him. The subjects were actors, but the decent people didn't know this. They thought they were punishing bad people. The experiment was done to prove that good people who were convinced by authority figures about the evil of others would hurt, even kill them. Human fears, ignorance, and prejudice enable leaders to get their followers to do anything to those whom they portray as enemies. Leaders are able to get people to commit atrocious acts against others by twisting information so that the enemy is no longer seen as a person like themselves.

Since you are the believed injured party it is up to you to communicate this to your persecutor. If he doesn't agree or understand and no one else can convince him, then you may be wrong or he is not emotionally ready to accept his behavior.

When someone hurts you he has diminished you in your own eyes, he has dehumanized you. It is easy to hurt him in an act of revenge without feeling remorse. If you do hurt him but you wish to grow as a person, you must recognize your mistake, and at that point you need to seek forgiveness. This is when you have the chance to redeem yourself. Ask him what you can do to be forgiven. If he is ready and can forgive you, you are in luck. Most of the time one of you remains out of rhythm with the other. You can still forgive yourself and, as I described, hope the other will eventually be ready. If not, you have emerged a healthier person.

If you're the real or believed victim, think about what it is that he can do which would make it possible for you to forgive him. Be true to your gut level feelings, but don't be further victimized by your own fears and pettiness. No matter what he finally does, if your forgiveness is sincere and you have risen above your pain, you will enjoy an ennobling experience which is an expression of your giant self.

I said forgiveness could be taught. I teach my students to respect and appreciate the humanity and intrinsic human worth of each of their classmates. I explain much of what this book is about and get them to understand and work with those who are different from them. I purposely group and alter these groupings. Many times after they have forged cohesive groups of six I tell them they have to get rid of one member. They are to use whatever method they wish, but one must be thrown out -- rejected! Most of the time if I've done a good job of teaching humanization skills they argue with me, get angry, or plead with me that they don't want to hurt anyone's feelings.

I get into my authoritarian role, demand they do it. I pound on the desks, yell, and have even threatened to paddle those groups who refuse. When the latter occurs, most give in and throw a child, a friend out of the group. I then point out what a terrible thing they have done to a classmate, to another human being. I am a good Jewish mother and everyone feels very guilty although the rationalizations they use are typical defense mechanisms.

Most apologize and make a concerted effort to be forgiven by the ones they rejected. Usually the rejected ones are those who have themselves been less than the best and most loyal of friends to the others. They all learn something valuable about friendship, loyalty, and forgiveness. Some move to even higher levels.

One year there was a revolution. The class refused to dehumanize their classmates. I ranted, raved, and threatened, but each time they refused to do it. I pounded the paddle on the desks in mock rage and they were terrified. One young fifth grade boy (no surprise that he's grown into an evolved adult) stood up and said in a trembling voice, "None of us are going to do this, it's wrong. We are not going to purposely hurt anyone's feelings!" Standing taller he announced, "We won't do this!"

The entire class sat frozen, scared, but together. It's been years, but every time I relate this story, I get teary-eyed with pride. It took me a moment to regain my composure, but I told them that each of them was on his way towards becoming a truly beautiful human being. I told them about Milgram's experiments and his cynicism. I said that most people are so afraid of authority they will sell their souls. I told them I knew how scared they were (which they acknowledged in relief), but, despite their fears, they had the courage and decency to protect others. They had stood together against a teacher whom they liked and feared, but who was trying to force them into doing an inhuman and cruel thing. I said that it was truly one of the highlights of my teaching career and no class would ever match what they did.

I had a few students before and after who refused, but never again an entire class. This shows that ethical-moral behavior can be taught to children or (adults) so that they can not be victimized by clever or cruel leaders. These children had been taught that there are reasons for the alleged bad or anti-social behavior of others. They had been taught to rethink the stereotypical reactions of their parents and society. They had been learning to forgive their classmates for their transgressions, even if they caused them pain or discomfort. They had been taught to forgive and they had done so under frightening conditions.

There can be no forgiveness without going through the crucible of pain and suffering. Forgiveness, like any other growth, means thought and learning how to deal with your pain. Although the greatest risks often provide the greatest opportunities for growth, it is not necessary to survive great tragedies such as Viktor Frankl did in a concentration camp. His psychiatrist's training and courage enabled him to learn that suffering was as important to growth as eating. However, suffering alone is not ennobling or growth-producing. Being human assures you of some suffering. The point is to use, to learn from the suffering, that is, to find meaning in it. If you are to grow, forgiveness is an integral part of that meaning.

I was turned off by neurolinguistic programming (NLP) even though I found it stimulating and brilliantly conceived. One of the leaders promised that you'd never have to suffer again, that by merely following the concepts of NLP you'd be able to solve all your problems. I had heard that hogwash so often in psychology, education, and other disciplines that it totally turned me off.

I agree with Rollo May, Frankl, Jung, de Chardin, and many others who realized that pain and suffering are a part of the human condition as much as happiness and joy. They saw that pain and suffering need not be searched out, but when they occur, they should be used as growth opportunities. These snake oil people who contribute to the anesthetizing of the human condition are not user friendly. They encourage you to believe that there are simple solutions to life's pain and complexity. Don't believe it.

A life lived fully will be filled with risks and errors. If you live your life as sensibly, completely, and rationally as you can you will avoid many mistakes those who don't do these things will suffer from. You will still experience pain and suffering. Anesthetizing yourself or deluding yourself just makes your problems worse. Some are caused by people, events, or organizations, over which you have little or no control, however much you believe that your powers, voice, or vote may matter. (Of course, your vote does.)

It is the way in which you handle your suffering that will determine your emotional/spiritual growth. Suffering stupidly or unnecessarily will not produce growth but merely perpetuate stupidity. The suffering should be redirected towards learning to transcend your genetically given and learned pettiness, greed, and selfishness. Your growth is determined by your ability to understand and love others even though their actions have caused you suffering. The ability to forgive them raises you above your diminished self and releases the greatness locked within.

As you practice forgiveness you find yourself slipping back (remember, there are no easy solutions) into anger and hostility, because people will continue to irritate you. This is the result of your brain's inability to totally erase, to forget the suffering that person or others have consciously or unconsciously caused you. Here's where practicing forgiveness pays off in combating stress and useless preoccupation with the past. Here's where your emotional/spiritual will and strength are necessary. This is where your giant self can assert itself and grow.

I have read of many people who through acts of will and courage have risen above their fears and pain and have forgiven their real and believed oppressors. I have experienced this in small and large ways in my life. These have been transcendent experiences which is why I say that forgiveness is divine.

Thirty-Nine

Love As An Answer

When I speak of love I will not be referring to unconditional love. I believe those who talk about unconditional love are speaking mythologically about gods, God, or someone who is not human. I do not believe that human beings can transcend their own need to love another without getting something in return. That something may not be tangible, but each individual who loves another is receiving something of value to him.

God's love is allegedly unconditional, but he has gone from a punishing god to one who forgives us everything. In exchange he demands our love and loyalty which is hardly unconditional. Instead of unconditional love I think humans should work towards a love that is just, has reasonable demands which can be achieved, and should be one that enhances the life of the loved one as well as oneself.

In the context of a giant self, love should be generative and transformative. It should encourage and enable you to go beyond what you thought possible for yourself. It should help make your life meaningful and help you to cope more effectively with your fears and weaknesses. And, as the lover, you should be able to do the same for your loved one. Although not unconditional, you should be able to accept and forgive the errors of those you love more easily than you can the lapses of others.

The word love has been trivialized by using it to describe anyone or anything pleasing to us. People speak of loving a dessert in the same way they refer to loving their spouses. Manfred Clynes in "Touch of Emotions," claims that the emotion of love, like other emotions, can be shown by sensitive instruments to display similar neuro-physiological patterns no matter what the culture. However, a person's interpretation and expression of these feelings will differ greatly. I know people will continue to say they love their animals, cars, hobbies, foods, in the same way they love their spouses. In the context of this chapter I will be encouraging you to apply the word love only to the process of loving another human being and how this process can enhance the development of both of your giant selves.

Remember the giant self is not an end product, but a process of total human growth. It is a constant development and unfolding of your potential. Every person will be at different levels in the actualization of these potentials, one of which is the ability to love and be loved.

I know it's easier for me to give love than accept it. It was a source of pain for my ex-wife, because she wanted to show me more love than I felt I deserved and so I rejected many of her attempts to please me. It was something I didn't learn to deal with then and it has been a problem with Marie who lives to shower her love on those she loves. It made me realize that reciprocity means being able to accept love without embarrassment as well as giving it.

Love is an energy force akin to nuclear fusion. Fission is the breaking apart of energy, fusion is putting it together. Love's amazing power is that the more of it you give away, the more is returned. It seems to follow its own laws of nature. This is the basis of my belief that the more people you love without hurting your primary relationship, the more love you create for everyone you love. The greater your capacity for love, with all the reciprocal responsibilities this entails, the more deeply you can love each loved one. The greater my love for Marie, the more I can love my children and my close friends, male or female.

My fondest and most powerful early memories are of my grandfather and grandmother. I vividly remember sitting between them in the synagogue. Both were always kind, physically affectionate, and totally accepting. They almost made me believe in unconditional love, but I was such a goody-goody that I never tested it. I never did anything to make them angry with me, (but then I only lived with them until I was seven.)

I used to do everything I could to help my grandmother around the house. She made me feel that I was useful and important and that I was capable of doing anything successfully. Around her I felt that I was very unique. So, I dusted, did dishes, vacuumed, and listened to all the radio soap operas with her. I loved her and to me she was beautiful. I hugged and kissed her, and sat on her lap any time I could. The women I loved should have been like her because of this early imprinting.

My grandmother was extremely overweight and not very attractive at all, yet I loved her. The women I dated and havebeen physically attracted to had attractive to beautiful faces and the bodies to match. I even told Marie that if she ever got fat I'd leave her. Although this was a statement which showed a superficiality that I was not proud of, it reflected a deep and real insecurity. Obviously, this critical attitude came later, after my uncritical love for my grandmother. It was the result of our cultural propaganda and education which emphasizes the external, the temporary, and the superficial rather than character and the internal person.

After my divorce I dated many women and twice I lived with women in an effort to understand what I needed and/or wanted. Several who said that they were in love with me were intelligent, sensitive, and any one of them would have been a good wife. To me none were as attractive as me ex. None could handle my daughters. I finally admitted I needed a woman who was beautiful -- because my ego (insecurity) was tied to that -- but she also had to be a good mother. Marie was beautiful, handled my two and her three children with ease, was the most passionate and exciting woman I'd ever met, and somehow communicated the same kind of feeling of unconditional love my grandmother had managed to give.

My grandmother died when I was seven and I moved away from my grandparents' home where I'd felt secure and loved unconditionally. My mother became my central figure. To me she looked like Rita Hayworth. I had a different standard of beauty by then. As with grandmother, I did everything I could to make her happy. She was very affectionate, loving, and I felt very loved. I was blessed.

My grandfather, and in later years, my father, were also loving and affectionate. With my father though, I felt fear, awe, and anger. I was finally overcoming these when he died. I was nineteen. A thoughtful, loving, interested uncle and two aunts made me the recipient of an abundance of love. Until I was eight I was the only child they all shared. In return I gave much to all of them. I was a loving, thoughtful, and courteous child. Up until then I had known only Jewish people and had not known the gut-wrenching rejection from non-Jews which almost destroyed my capacity to love myself or others.

In my earliest relationships I was taught how to love and be loved. There were many commonalties of loving shared by those who first taught me. Many of these were characteristics of those I selected to be my closest friends and lovers.

My love experiences are not to be construed as some sort of shopping list so you can compare yours with mine to determine how much you love or can be loved; or to determine whether you are in love with someone or he/she loves you. Each person's ability to love and be loved is very different. A person may not score high on my analysis of what it takes, but may either be or become a loving person. Further, the generative and transformative powers of love may cause an almost instantaneous change; or such change may take much time. A flower doesn't bloom for nothing. Build your base. Think and learn about these factors. Experience love by reaching out, risking, and attempting deeper and more fulfilling relationships. Begin with accepting and understanding your parents, then your friends, and finally those you are capable of growing towards and with. The order of these factors doesn't relate to their importance. All are important and must fit your needs and abilities.

As a child I did things wrongly or badly and I was punished. Although I suffered the consequences I was not made to feel inherently bad or unlovable. I was pretty well accepted with all my faults.

Still, it's very difficult to be accepting of another person's faults. His faults mess up your plans or complicate your life. My grandparents and parents were trying to make me perfect. Of course, they reinforced behaviors to socialize me which weren't always the most healthy, such as determining my worth by the amount of food I ate or the size of my bowel movement. Many of the other behaviors encouraged in socializing a child are totally inappropriate and intolerable in a relationship between adults.

All of us want to be accepted as we are, warts and all as the expression goes. This is the ideal of unconditional love. Unconditional love happens rarely to anyone as a child and is impossible in an adult relationship. There is usually a double standard. You want unconditional love and total acceptance from the other, but you are only able to accept him with quite specific conditions. It is similar to a one-sided prenuptial agreement.

Both want the other to change for the sake of the relationship. This isn't too damaging if you are both willing to admit you have faults that are irritating to the other. You admit you cannot accept him/her totally without some changes, some compromises. Acceptance is then placed on a basis of very specific limitations. Each of you must be willing to work towards making these changes. As they occur and the partner's life is made more pleasant, then she/he is more willing to make further compromises, as you will be. In the joy you feel while being together you will want to continue to make these healthy changes, i. e. if they are reasonable and possible. However, if these changes diminish you, then this is not an expression of love but of fear on the part of the other.

Example: Jealousy. I know of a young woman who gets angry when her lover looks at other women. It is so bad that he cannot even admire women in movies. If he makes any comment about their beauty, she gets hysterical and cries. This is an extreme, but demonstrates the unhealthy kinds of compromises and changes people expect. It is an example of an attempt at manipulation, not compromise. I would consider it a healthy request on his part for her to get therapy for her sick jealousy.

Acceptance does not mean unconditional love. It does not mean accepting every negative, hostile, or stupid thing she/he does. These all need to be faced and dealt with. It does mean accepting frailties and weaknesses if there is a sincere attempt to grow towards expressions of the giant self. It means temporarily accepting your partner's faults while she/he is consciously trying to improve.

After all, this is what you want also. While you are groping with your attempts to create your giant self you what to be accepted and loved. Neither of you should expect unconditional love because it's unattainable. If both of you can work towards making the goals of your love reachable, you increase your chances of improving yourselves and your relationship. The more specific and clearly you understand your needs and expectations and the more each is willing to compromise, the more complete your love will become.

Love grows through reciprocity. Manipulation is one-sided and leaves one feeling cheated. Love grows when a person knows what is expected of him and then he is rewarded by having some of his needs met. Love grows when he makes a mistake which you are able to forgive because you believe he is risking and improving.

Acceptance is allowing her to make mistakes without her feeling you're going to hate or leave her. It means listening to what is important to her and responding appropriately. It is physically showing your love because your passion, interest, and concern for her body and feelings speak louder than any other means of acceptance.

I know of excellent and loving relationships between people with little sex or physical displays of affection involved. I think this is rare and I'm not sure these are as good as they report. A couple may have settled for this because they don't think they can get more from their spouse. For most people, the more fully and totally they are accepted by their spouse, the more alive and happy they are. For most people to be sexually accepted by another is a major measure of value and worth. Lack of a sense of acceptance is one of the main reasons relationships deteriorate.

Individual differences as well as genetic differences between males and females create a constant source of potential rejection. It is usually the male who initially feels rejection because his sexual needs are more easily met in brief encounters than hers are. As time goes on the female, with her physiological need for more time spent talking, foreplay, and physical reassurance and love afterwards, is increasingly disappointed, rejected, and feels unaccepted.

By understanding and learning about the other's needs and realizing that they are always changing and different, the couple can find solutions which will increase their mutual and conditional acceptance of each other. By making it clear that the relationship is conditional each knows that he/she must continue to be alert towards making the compromises necessary for each to maximize the strength of the relationship in a context which also maximizes each one's own potentials for growth. This approach is not poetic or idealistic, but practical.

As a child the things I did to show my love were appreciated. My family told and showed me that I was loved, but there were specific reinforcements so I knew what I had to do to show love and to get more love. I expect my wife, children, or anyone to whom I express love to be responsive and show their appreciation. I thank the students I teach and they learn to return my appreciation of specific deeds. My wife and family physically express their appreciation toward me as I do toward them. I expect this and would demand it if it didn't spontaneously spring forth from all of us. However, it did not just happen, but is the result of years of conscious effort of showing appreciation of things which pleased us.

Those who expect but don't get unconditional love and appreciation are probably those who seldom express their appreciation of what their loved ones do for them.

The various manifestations of appreciation glowingly emerge from those who are loved and appreciated by another. In the beginning of a relationship you should be knocking yourself out for ways to tell and show your loved one how much love you're feeling. I could hardly contain myself in the beginning of a relationship. I wanted to spend every moment with her. I wanted to give her everything I could. I doted on her because her eyes, voice, and body told me in countless ways how much she loved me. I felt loved and appreciated.

With Marie the passion that inflamed and made us feel more totally appreciated than any time in our lives still exists. It has had its ebb and flow, its times when the conditions for appreciation were not met, but each major crises has strengthened our love.

As I was growing up my family and I showed reciprocity in our love. I could not reciprocate at the levels of love they could, because I was immature. I was learning the give and take necessary for love. You need to take stock of your lover's ability to reciprocate. Is she unable to express love because she's never received it and doesn't know how to act? If you love her and she's never known love, but despite her fears she is willing to risk and learn, then keep giving and gently, but patiently encourage her as she tries to be loving. Expecting too much will make her feel like a failure and she will give up. Your level of loving and maturity will also determine how long you can give without much reciprocity. Without some reciprocity you will feel (and be) used, not loved.

So-called unrequited love is love without reciprocity. It is a romantic fiction created by people who are lacking in passion and have little self-confidence. The loved one is idealized and no demands are made upon him/her so both live in a fantasy fueled by the inability to risk. This is not love, it is pretentious cowardice.

Reciprocity entails responsibility. When you love someone you are partially responsible for your lover's happiness as she/he is for yours. You are not totally responsible because that would cripple both of you! You because you were expected to be all and the other because nothing would be demanded in return.

When you choose to share your life you owe more than mere reciprocity. You accept some of the responsibility for the happiness and welfare of the other person.

This does not mean that either should be a burden upon the other: love should be joy. You should want to be together, learn about and want to please and care for the beloved to the best of your ability. For lovers there is not at first any conscious sense of responsibility because they cannot seem to do enough for each other. If this impulse is missing I seriously doubt it it's love.

As you mature and your roles are clarified then your areas of mutual responsibility are understood consciously as will as unconsciously.

My father and one aunt were the only ones who, at times in my preschool years, made me withdraw. With others I could express the full range of my emotions. I could express myself without fearing it would be used against me. I loved classical music and used to dance about the living room. My aunt referred to my movements as clumsy and elephantine; my father inferred I was effeminate. I became a boxer rather than a dancer because of their looks and statements. I withheld parts of me from them because I couldn't trust my vulnerabilities to them.

This lack of trust, the refusal to be vulnerable around others is why many people cannot experience a deep and profound love. Deep love means opening yourself to the other. You are naked and exposed. If she is hostile or nonloving she can strike a damaging or even fatal blow to your ability to love.

To those I've loved I've opened up and trusted and risked that they would reciprocate. The first one to say "I love you," is risking enormous rejection or the greatest high. In the process I have been cruelly hurt and rejected. I have as well dealt killing blows. Sometimes I was rejected because I believed I had not been accepted; I struck out in blind, vicious hostility. In my anguish and stupidity I have deeply hurt those I loved and vice-versa. Through it all I have come to believe strongly that the more trusting and vulnerable I am, the deeper my relationship can be. It is a calculated risk, but well worth it.

However, I do not bare my soul immediately to anyone. It is a gradual unveiling. Through reciprocity we gradually accept each other's faults, show appreciation for the fears and strengths of the other, and demonstrate a sense of responsibility for the care and welfare of the other.

Opening oneself up is a terrifying thing to do because it is so risky. That's why most people either don't experience love or its powers get so overwhelming that they withdraw and lose what they had or could have had.

Love is not love until it has stood the test of time. I believe in passion and chemistry. Love at first sight and the grand passion go together for me, but unless they can be sustained over time and the love flowers and both parties are working towards developing their giant selves, it is not truly human love, merely animal attraction. (That ain't bad, but it ain't love.) What is called love could have matured into real love if both parties had dealt with each other's problems in an accepting, responsible manner.

There have been several women in my life whom I thought I loved or who said they loved me, but our relationships were short-lived because of unfinished business we brought into the situation. Even when a relationship broke up, I seldom suffered the agony I experienced from my grandmother's and father's deaths or the loss of my girls through my divorce.

I can't believe it can be called love if the person can be replaced like a pet dog. I see people who are "in love" several times a year. Once in a lifetime is enough for many, a few times for most. The loss of too many love relationships can be severely traumatic.

If after years the loved person remains in your heart, dreams, and thoughts and you continue to wish to be with her, that's love. After a quarter of a century I still look forward to seeing Marie whether I'm returning from work or she's on her way back from the store. I enjoy her company. This had stood the test of time.

Marie knows I am joyful, happy to be with her, because I constantly tell her so. Whenever I come home and her car isn't in the driveway, my heart drops. I enjoy being with her because we can laugh at our mistakes and weaknesses, especially the other one's. We both mug a lot, talk in a strange lingo known only to us, and generally act silly.

Laughter has always been a part of my love relations. It's one of the things women have found attractive because it's a key element which relieves the day-to-day tedium of life. Stable relationships are based on routine, but routine tends to get boring at times. Laughter eases this.

This laughter does not have to be the hostile "Who's Afraid of Virginia Woolf?" type which is a sadomasochistic intellectual-emotional sparring match. I've been in those. I enjoyed them at the time because I was hurting and the process of punishing another person was temporarily distracting and relieving. In these situations the hostilities continue because neither one listens to the other, but the pain does become cumulative. The same stupid accusations are used to bludgeon the other until love turns to depression, despair, and/or hate.

Recently, Marie and I found ourselves trapped in one of these vicious cycles. We entered into therapy but the real change came when both admitted we were in a trap, stopped playing old tapes and worked towards livable compromises. Usually we can cut through smoke screens and get to the guts of a problem. Then either a compromise is reached or, if there is no solution (and despite what some experts say, there are problems which are insoluble), then we grit our teeth and live with the discomfort and pain.

We use humor to deal with these problems because it works. It works because we realize that we need to be self-protective at times and are covering up from our fears and insecurities, not from a lack of love for the other. Since we know and can admit we are weak and frightened, we can give in, knowing we don't have to be infallible. Nor do we expect to have all our needs met. Our fairly constant joy in being together and our ability to see ourselves and others (especially others) in humorous ways enables our love to flourish.

Our joy is usually quite simple. We don't need to go to extravagant places or do exotic things (and couldn't afford too) because we can share the beauty of our gardens, the clever things our children say and grandchildren do (to others), and our conversations. Joy is holding hands in the movies and getting most of the popcorn. It is listening to her infectious laugh (at my stories) and her passion in bed.

I know of couples, friends, and families who communicate their love through nonverbal or silent ways. This does not work for me. Most women I've known and loved wanted a lot of verbal communication as well as affection and passion. Generally, men do not need or desire as much verbal communication. A man who can listen the way a woman wants him to is in great demand.

Talking is one of the main ways we are qualitatively different from other animals. We can express what goes on in our minds, hearts, and souls verbally and nonverbally. Through these expressions we discover parts of ourselves often hidden to us. A loving partner can bring our hidden qualities out. Without this we remain locked within a diminished self and it dominates our lives. The diminished self is incapable of healthy communication, of love as I am defining it.

I do not believe love can develop without communication and I know it can't survive. There are many psychological, social, cultural, and physiological reasons why a person cannot communicate. If he can't, he cannot have a fully developed love. How can he know what she wants from him or vice-versa? He must be able to understand her needs if he is going to be able to meet them.

When I first met Marie I devoted myself to her night and day. I thought continuously about what she wanted and needed and I anticipated her wishes. She reciprocated. The reciprocity is created and enhanced through communication.

This involves much more than knowing what she wants to eat or drink. It means studying her and then increasing your vulnerability and exposure so you know her inner life. It takes time, training, and effort to do this. It definitely means you must trust and be trusted. Because it is risky most people acting from their diminished selves can't trust enough to do this. They have learned not to trust. Unfortunately, this means they are unable to give or receive love.

I am human (therefore) I am weak and vulnerable. I can communicate this to my partner without her seeing me as a weakling. (This knowledge took a crisis which almost destroyed us, but I learned and admitted my fears and insecurities after years of a smooth cover-up.) The more honest I am, the more honest she will be with me. This does ease some of the insoluble problems mentioned. Marie and I disagree on religion, sexual freedom, and how long to barbecue the meat. We have come to the realization that when we're discussing these issues we need to keep very calm and not step on the other's toes. I have gotten furious when she tells people that I really do believe in the Judeo-Christian God and she seldom says this anymore. She has gotten unnecessarily hurt by my anti-religious statements which she took as put-downs of her.

When we communicate in sensitive areas we try to respect the other's feelings and intelligence. We know that honesty is important and each should feel comfortable in expressing divergent views, but there is a thin line between honesty and cruelty. We also recognize we each want to be right, to get in the last word. At times this is not communication; it is the diminished self afraid it is wrong. We still try to convince each other of the correctness of our beliefs, but carefully watch the other and usually know when to let it rest.

In our country it seems to me more important to be right than to be loved. Marie and I have compromised so we can express different ideas, but know when to shut up. When we don't there is a useless argument. You can tell the difference because communication means listening to the other; an argument is two people talking without a listener. Arguments are notable in that each tediously repeats the same thing over and over because he knows the others isn't listening. The other has heard the arguments, but doesn't agree.

We used to argue fruitlessly until we realized that we were communicating our positions quite clearly, but the other just didn't agree. From this came frustration and finally the agreement that although we couldn't or wouldn't agree we could still love one another. This was a major breakthrough.

It is my right to think and feel anything I want. It is not my right to try to force my thoughts or feeling on Marie, not hers to force anything on me. It is neither respectful nor responsible. Some matters I discuss with others because these things would only needlessly upset her; she does the same. It's true it would be great if we could be totally honest, but that would mean we were in absolute agreement. If we agreed on everything we would bore each other to death.

The expression of my love comes from listening to and appreciating her fears as well as her strengths. Each of us found areas of pain or disagreement. We continue to explore then, but with sensitivity. I do not have to like or love her fears, but I have to respect them if I want her to respect mine. I must respect her right to her fears and frailties. I am granted this right in return. What we are really saying is that we can live with the weaknesses of the other and still be loving. It means that our giant selves can accept the other's humanness. To achieve this acceptance may mean a drastic change in how you have viewed communication. But it will make your relationship much healthier.

Marie and others have commented on how much kinder I am than when I was in my thirties and forties. I have always treated people courteously, but if they mistreated me I gave as good as I got.

I had trouble with kindness because I felt unappreciated and blamed others for my lack of success. I was hurt by life and withdrew except when I poked my head out to bite someone. I was however, different with my family and those I taught.

I no longer spend my time uselessly blaming others. I am kind to everyone and usually receive kindness in return. In my intimate relationships I am kinder and this has made my life much more peaceful. I believe if you were kinder with your loved ones you'd see a quick and lasting change in your relationships.

As I said previously forgiveness is very difficult because the memories of the alleged wrong is forever embedded in your brain/body. However, the more you can forgive and live in the present, the easier it will be to forget much of the pain so that your relationships can survive. If you cannot forgive, and many cannot because of their weak, diminished selves, then your relationships will probably sicken and die.

Loving is the attempt to understand and live with difficult differences. The more honest you are, the greater will your differences be because you risk exposing them. The greater your love, the more you can adjust to differences.

These differences can cause situations in which one person sees the other as cruel, bad, or thoughtless. It is difficult to forgive someone when you're in pain or are disappointed. Believing you can forgive is the first step. Thinking and trying to understand the other is the second. Acting on your forgiveness is the third and hardest step. You are fighting your own fears and don't want to appear foolish in the eyes of others. You also don't want to be taken advantage of again.

The is where your giant self takes over. It isn't preoccupied with blame, but in making the present better. It should help you be wary, but not paranoid. If there are no changes in the other and he continues to behave in a manner you can't live with -- don't! Usually in a marriage though, your partner will feel your sincerity and efforts and this allows his/her giant self to emerge. Like any other character trait, forgiveness is developed through practice, through specific acts demonstrating forgiveness.

You may think you cannot forgive, but by reorganizing your thinking, you may surprise yourself. Let your giant self operate in this arena.

Daily existence with its need for order and harmony tends to be repetitious. Repetition can lead to sameness and boredom, boredom to disinterest, disinterest to things that are more stimulating.

Love needs mystery. It needs the unexpected. As people grow they make unexpected changes. These changes can be the spark, they can give mystery to your love. The loved person is no longer totally predictable. This unpredictably can come from the different interests you each pursue or from new ways of seeing the things commonly shared. Changed perceptions can come from your primary relationship or from some of your secondary ones.

Marie says that she is sometimes uncomfortable with my unpredictability, but she also finds it stimulating and it keeps her interested. I don't plan to be unpredictable, but unforeseen changes emanate from my explorations of my giant self as I read, think, act, and write.

Innovations do not need to be gigantic or extravagant, but must be unexpected. It's usually best if the surprise is something which springs from your relationship and is a new expression of your love. As your love deepens and each of you grows and expands your potentials, each of you will become more interesting and understandable. However, a part of you will always remain unfathomable and mysterious.

Love creates an amazing paradox. The more you are loved and loving the more you realize your uniqueness. Your love makes you feel there is no one on earth like you. You feel special. You are overwhelmed with your abundance of good feelings, intelligence, and strength which allow your giant self to be expressed kaleidoscopically. Strangely enough, this giant you that feels its uniqueness so strongly, is simultaneously able to blend happily into a unique entity with the loved one. This is holographic. Although the love relationship surrounds and includes both of you inclusively, you remain a separate person exclusively with an increasingly clear-cut identity of your own.

In physics particles paradoxically seem to manifest both energy and mass. Light both has a wave and a particle reality. Love makes you one and two at the same time. It destroys the sense of separateness from the other and makes you feel a oneness which is the end of isolation and aloneness. Yet love makes you feel extraordinarily unique. You are unique, she is unique, and so is the relationship. There is a you, a her, and an us.

To seemingly lose yourself is to end the alienation and loneliness humans experience -- the alienation which create the "existential dilemma" about the alleged "meaningless of life." Love not only gives meaning to life, it is its greatest expression. The companionship that turns two separate humans into a totally different life force is an expression of love's generative and transformative character. This life force or force field is exponentially transformative because of is unlimited potential to positively affect everything and everyone it touches. Love transforms persons, families, friends, organizations, and countries in an ever widening expansiveness.

The most effective love relationships have balance. They mix planning with spontaneity, honesty with kindness, self-centeredness with other-centeredness. They balance the physical, mental, emotional, and social facets of human life. The spiritual facet also needs to be considered. I know most people place it on the top of a hierarchy. I don't. Each of the factors interacts with all the others. They have different intensities, usefulness, and values at different moments of your life. No human works at each with equal vigor, but many problems occur because one or more overbalances the others leaving the person unbalanced. It's easy for others to notice when one factor is dominating a person's life. We call him fanatic, crazy, or some such label which means he is out of synch, off balance. Just as your sexual self cannot be adequately expressed until certain physical changes occur, your spiritual self cannot be well-developed until you achieve a level of mental and emotional maturity and your vision of the world becomes cosmic. (Children have a spiritual side or self, but like their bodies, it needs different nourishment as it's developing.)

Your spiritual self makes you into a cosmic ecologist. It should help you see yourself, others, institutions, the world, and then the universe in a gigantic perspective in which you play a small but significant part. Spirituality helps balance the incessant demands of your ego and encourages you to be increasingly interdependent. It is crucial in dealing with loneliness, meaninglessness, and alienation. The form your spirituality takes is not as relevant as the quest itself.

Spirituality, like all the necessary ingredients of your giant self, is a lifelong searching, testing, and flowering of your human potentials. And, although a person can be both religious and spiritual, my bias is that it is better to be spiritual then religious. A balanced spiritual person could never be a party to the inhuman cruelties that religious people have perpetrated on others.

A truly balanced spiritual person would be an outstanding candidate for a lasting love sex relationship because he would not let his fears and pettiness become impediments to loving the other. A person with a spiritual, cosmic view would see that the more he enhances the potentials of his love and of others, the more everyone grows.

Caution. If your partner doesn't satisfy the demands of one or more of these factors don't dump her or him and look for the perfect one. There ain't no such person and you ain't perfect either! These factors were explained to give you some guidelines to help you improve and understand your self, your beloved, and your relationship.

These are my realities. Many other realities for me are not only probable, they are desirable. I'm certain as I grow I'll change my views. (From the first edition of this book in 1983 until now, I changed many things.) Since I'm a believer in the unavoidability of certain kinds of errors, of human fragility and fallibility, maybe this whole book is a mistake. (I don't believe it.)

Love is your (our) reason for existence. The development and release of your giant self is the way to achieve love with all its levels and permutations. It's like the genie locked in the bottle: love and your giant self are waiting to emerge. Open up to them!

Forty

Glossary Of Fanciful Fictions

ACCULTURATION: The changes that occur in both cultures when two of them meet. The same happens when two people or sets of families have constant contact. Both change, for better and worse.

COMPETITION: A clever motivational device which keeps you striving for unattainable goals. This device insures failure, and keeps you unbalanced and vulnerable (so you will do whatever your leaders ask.) It cripples you and your competitors because it means insatiability and a no-win situation. It is Hell's treadmill with Heavenly trappings.

COMPROMISE: What you want the other person to give up while you get your way. A temporary state in which neither person gets what he wants as each tries to get more than his fair share.

CULTURE: A human-made group of values, practices, and organizations which is created to meet our many physical, mental, social, emotional, and spiritual needs. In return each culture controls our thoughts, feelings, and behaviors homogenizing our mind and limiting many choices while expanding others.

DEFERRED JUDGEMENT: A technique perfected by Sidney Parnes to counteract the natural tendency of your brain to make instant judgements based on insufficient data.

DIMINISHED SELF: The little person that culture makes you because you cannot satisfy its insatiable appetite to make you meet its complex demands. Your diminished self makes you mean, petty, and small-minded. You see or encourage the worst in others and enjoy diminishing them.

EGOHOLISM: A condition of self-intoxication and delusion in which your fears and insecurities are so overwhelming that you cannot understand nor try to meet anyone else's needs.

EITHER/OR LOGIC: A rigidity of feeling, thinking, or acting, based on fear and stupidity, which results in tunnel vision. An inability to see

214

alternatives or shadings. You see everything as absolutely black or white.

ETHNOCENTRISM: Egoholism on a tribal, group, or national scale. Selfishness resulting in long-term damage to the world's physical, social, emotional, and spiritual ecosystems.

EVIL: Anything that slows, reverses, or stops healthy growth.

FEAR: What I experienced when I realized who might read this book, or worse, what I'd feel if no one did. Your giant self uses fear as a signal of danger and uses its resources to confront it realistically. It is an expression of your diminished self when it prevents you from doing what your believe is ethical and beneficial to you or others.

FREEDOM: An imaginary commodity that you never seem to get enough of for yourself because you are busily preoccupied in limiting it for others.

GIANT SELF: The totality of all your potentials. It is the out-flowing of talents and skills which make you human and godlike, but is trampled upon by cultural controls (the collective diminishers) and your diminished self. It is enhanced and freed by love, will, and courage.

GOD: That which is defined as Infinite, Ineffable, All-Powerful, Always Present, and Unknowable. A means to logically explain what is not explainable. A term used by finite, weak, and frightened humans to explain what they've done or about to do to you for your own good, but which leaves you confused, diminished, battered, or dead.

GUILT: Culture's device for making you feel ashamed and diminished for doing what your mind and body were created to do. Guilt may be productive if used as a signal that something should be changed.

HUMOR: A device to release the tension caused by your humanness and fallibility. A way to keep your sense of perspective and emotional balance and to counteract what the diminishers do to you daily. A non-toxic hallucinogenic drug which helps you see a healthier, alternative reality.

INTUITION: A felt sense within your body which, if allowed to be expressed and developed, is a balance and an equal to logic. It is equally liable to human error.

LINEARITY: A step-by-step mechanical line of events or information processing. One of the ways your brain operates. Like intuition, it is liable to many types of errors.

LOGIC: A sometimes useful method of information processing. Held in high esteem by minds afraid to risk and be creative. Mediocre minds believe it is the only way to avoid error and find truth.

LOVE: An invisible force that, in its highest expressions, unites diverse persons, enhances their small selves, and best promotes the development and expressions of their giant selves. It is the power that activates and generates symbiosis and synthesis.

MARRIAGE: A legal contract binding two people who could be friends and lovers into a situation of unrealistic demands and expectations in which their complex physical, mental, emotional, and spiritual needs cannot be fully explored nor met. May also be the evolutionary next step, in spite of its possibilities for mutual growth having been hampered by sexism, jealousy, possessiveness, and other negatives stemming from diminished selves.

PAIN: Whether physical, mental, emotional, or spiritual, pain is a useful indicator of something gone wrong. Merely anesthetizing pain inhibits its usefulness, and loses its messages.

PERFECTION: What you expect from your mate, children, friends, others, and occasionally from yourself, ensuring that you or anyone else is never satisfied with anyone's efforts.

PERSONALIZING: The tendency to take everything that happens as an indicator that others or malevolent forces are always working against you. Egotistical nonsense, except for the times when I can prove some of you have been unfairly and unjustly out to get me.

PERSONAL MYTH: The totality of erroneous beliefs about yourself that are insanely defended by you and tend to create or perpetuate myths which are not consistent with the historical events.

POSSESSIVENESS: Your efforts to control other persons for your uses or gains without considering their needs.

REALITY: The world according to Garp. Or me. Or even you!

RESONANCE: A rhythm of mood, feeling, and/or thought and action which occurs during times when mutual respect and love for yourself and an-other or others causes two or more harmonies to blend into one, creating a unity.

SCIENCE: A clever semantic device and method to replace God as a means to explain and cope with the Mysterious and Unexplainable. Its advocates, like religious men, wear uniforms and make up their own rules, laws, languages, and rituals to disguise their ignorance and bamboozle the Uninitiated.

SECURITY: A delusion emanating deep within your diminished self which reflects your fears of death, meaninglessness, alienation, and loneliness. To begin the creation of your giant self you must gradually accept the fact that uncertainty and insecurity go hand in glove with being human.

SIMULTANEITY: Many things happening at once. Another way your brain operates. This is difficult to accept and deal with, so most of us try to pretend that everything is logical and linear.

TRADE-OFFS: Consciously choosing among alternatives while knowing full well that you won't get everything you want. Accepting your losses while appreciating your gains.

UNFINISHED BUSINESS: All the unsaid and undone things that keep jangling around in your brain/body which you have not honestly faced, dealt with, or cannot complete and which constantly undermine the growth of your giant self.